JANET S. STEINWEDEL, PhD

GROUP COACHING

Raising Leadership Consciousness, Effectiveness, and Engagement in Organizations

I0119134

The Art and Practice of Facilitating Leadership Development Cohorts

Book 3 in the Steinwedel Red Book Series

CHIRON PUBLICATIONS • ASHEVILLE, NORTH CAROLINA

www.ChironPublications.com

Third in the Steinwedel Red Book Series
Cover design and book typesetting by Cornelia G. Murariu
Cover artwork by Mariá Eva Trajterová, "Brana," new gate or path: Your truth opens the gate to the consciousness of everybody

Printed primarily in the United States of America.

ISBN 978-1-63051-744-1 paperback
ISBN 978-1-63051-745-8 hardcover
ISBN 978-1-63051-746-5 electronic
ISBN 978-1-63051-747-2 limited edition paperback

Library of Congress Cataloging-in-Publication Data

Names: Steinwedel, Janet S., author.
Title: Group coaching : raising leadership consciousness, effectiveness,
    and engagement in organizations : the art and practice of facilitating
    leadership development cohorts / Janet S. Steinwedel, PHD. Description:
Asheville : Chiron Publications, 2020. | Series: Steinwedel
    red book series ; Book 3 | Includes bibliographical references. |
Summary: "Janet Steinwedel's work with groups aims for a net increase in
consciousness in the organization or community in which she is working.
This is the third book in the Steinwedel Red Book Series-a series
    focused on the integration of Jungian psychology and executive coaching.
In this book she explains her collaboration with organizations to choose
    a handful of leaders who will benefit from a focus on enhancing their
leadership. Janet has focused on balancing the goals side of the
    coaching process with aspiration and inspiration in an effort to support
clients on their path to individuation and wholeness. She has worked
    with many leaders that have been nudged out of alignment with their
values and lose their passion for their work and her process is designed
    to bring that alignment back"-- Provided by publisher.
Identifiers: LCCN 2020016247 (print) | LCCN 2020016248 (ebook) | ISBN
    9781630517441 (paperback) | ISBN 9781630517458 (hardcover) | ISBN
    9781630517465 (ebook)
Subjects: LCSH: Executive coaching. | Employees--Coaching of. | Jungian
    psychology. | Leadership--Psychological aspects.
Classification: LCC HD30.4 .S7367 2020 (print) | LCC HD30.4 (ebook) | DDC
    658.4/07124--dc23
LC record available at https://lccn.loc.gov/2020016247
LC ebook record available at https://lccn.loc.gov/2020016248

Praise for *Group Coaching*

"Janet Steiwedel's book is a practical and inspirational guide for a group coach seeking to integrate programmatic group coaching with the best of the Jungian approach, integrating vision and meaning."

**Justin Hecht, PhD, Certified Jungian Analyst &
Certified Group Psychotherapist, San Francisco**

"My experience with Insight Group Coaching has been one of the most meaningful experiences of my career in medicine. As an introvert and an optimist, I was initially not sure how to react to one of my colleagues in the group who seemed very negative. As the months progressed I realized that her comments served as my guide, permitting me to look inside myself at thoughts and feelings being triggered in me, and I gained a deeper understanding of what was really holding me back as a leader. This direct opportunity for self-discovery under the guidance of our facilitator enabled me to see myself more clearly. In the end, self-awareness facilitated transformative growth and self acceptance."

**Linda J. Lang, MD, Chair, Department of Psychiatry, Behavioral
Health Service Line Health Care System**

"For twenty years my work as a Presbytery Executive was assisting congregations in managing change, particularly the transition of pastors. Over time the frequency and furor of these transitions accelerated and the systems in place to manage these changes became overwhelmed. The work Dr. Janet Steinwedel defines in this book offers a compelling and compassionate model of how regional church bodies might better support pastors in navigating constant change. This book does not propose to be a theological work. However, it does illuminate the human journey to better know oneself in order to better serve others in healthy and helpful ways. What strikes me in Dr. Steinwedel's writing as both obvious and yet tragically understated in leadership development is the critical need to support the interior work of self-discovery. Group Coaching provides a road map for establishing a coaching initiative which will resonate with clergy and have direct application to the practices of good pastoral work. Yet more than a road map, what is provided here is a vision for a healthy and vital organization which believes in the innate ability of people to grow in giftedness and grace. Thank you, Janet, for such an affirmation!"

**Reverend Jim Moseley, Campbell Memorial
Presbyterian Church, Weems, VA.**

"I found Janet's third book in her *Red Book Series* to be very thought-provoking. It is clear that she is a talented, experienced facilitator and coach who designs deceptively simple programs that increase the leadership capabilities and self-awareness of her participants. This simplicity belies the knowledge, the trials and errors, and the innate expertise that allowed her to create and facilitate such elegant initiatives. And, what is additionally wonderful is that Janet provides a blue print to others who support peoples' growth on how to develop impactful processes."

Barbara Taylor, Partner, JanBara Associates

"I was given the privilege to be a participant in a women's group led by Janet. The opportunity came at a nodal point in my own career as I was appointed to a prominent leadership position in the organizations' newly established service line structure. While not new to management, it was my first experience in that type of role. I welcomed the prospect of working so closely with women in similar positions within the organization."

"The experience was indeed transformative. The 'prework' of understanding myself as guided by testing and discussions with Janet provided the platform for working with the group. The sessions were masterfully conducted to allow each of us to attain a much deeper understanding of ourselves. That knowledge of our true selves enabled each of us to expand our appreciation of the intricacies of human interaction so that we felt empowered to more effectively navigate the often turbulent waters encountered in leadership positions."

"My journey since the sessions has had its own twists and turns, each one an opportunity for learning and growth. The insight gained through working with the group has brought me to an inner peace that continues to serve as the guiding principle in both my personal and professional life."

"I would like to congratulate Janet for writing this book and thank her for the invaluable contributions she continues to make through her work."

Elizabeth Zadzielski, MD, MBA, Chair, Department of Obstetrics and Gynecology, Sinai Hospital of Baltimore

Table of Contents

Acknowledgments

It is with a great deal of gratitude that I think of all of the colleagues, and friends who have provided me support in this endeavor. It would be impossible to acknowledge each by name. For those who pre-read the manuscript and provided feedback and endorsement, Harold Delhagen, Justin Hecht, Sandy Aman Keller, Dennis Slattery, Murray Stein, Barbara Taylor, Linda Lang, Jim Moseley, Elizabeth Zadzielski, I thank you dearly.

I am particularly grateful to my editor, Anne Dubuisson, for her insight and skillful approach in helping me bring out that which was most important in a way that made it readable. And to everyone at Chiron Publications, especially Jennifer Fitzgerald, Steve Buser, Len Cruz, Nelly Murariu and Rob Mikulak—thank you for believing in this series and supporting its development. It's been a pleasure working with you.

I am appreciative for so many teachers, mentors and guides who have showed up over the years—I especially want to thank, Sally Bell, Jim Hollis, Roger Housden, Alden Josey, and David Whyte, and all at the Philadelphia Jung Association (PAJA), and professors and friends at the Fielding Graduate University (FGU) who have been core to my growth and development.

And finally, my heartfelt thanks to my husband, Steve, who has enhanced my vision and my being through his curiosity and ongoing exploration of the psychospiritual world, and for the continuous encouragement of family and friends—I am indebted to you all.

To my groups with members around the world

I'm grateful to the people who have had the courage to sponsor a group in their organization.

May we all aim to be more aware in the world and to be more conscious of what is moving in and around and through us in an effort to bring more satisfaction to our work and our lives.

Preface

*"In the history of the collective, everything
depends on the development of consciousness."*

C. G. Jung

This is the third book in the Steinwedel Red Book Series. Carl Jung's *Red Book* was in service to his growth in consciousness and wholeness. In it he explores his own experiences at his most vulnerable period and captures what it means to really do the inner work needed to reposition the ego in an effort to meet the *Self*[1] and truly author one's unique life. This, too, is my charge, to truly discover who I am through my work, my choices, and my life and to engage in reflection on these things in order to make sense of them. I believe this is your work too. It is how we make an authentic and meaningful life and how we effectively support others on this journey.

The first book, *The Golden Key to Executive Coaching…And One Treasure Chest Every Coach Needs to Explore*, provided a basic understanding of Jungian psychology and demonstrated how I've integrated those ideas with my work as an executive coach. Results of that effort have been greater development of *Self,* my platform, and my skills; also, enhanced support of those I work with and an increased ability to encourage other coaches to commit to their inner work.

The second book in the series, *Authenticity as an Executive Coach: Waking Up the Wounded Healer Archetype,* built on the foundation provided

---

1   The Self is an archetypal notion of that which is me, but much greater than the ego me. Jung capitalized it to note the distinction. It is at the center of the psyche and it is the totality of the psyche. The ego is at the center of the conscious field. (Further commentary in books 1 and 2.)

in *The Golden Key* in order to focus more clearly on the problem of projection, transference and countertransference. It highlighted the *wounded healer* archetype to show how one's difficult experiences, especially early in life, play out for the executive coach (teacher, pastor, counselor … those in the support professions) in their work. It demonstrated that when we learn to observe ourselves, to witness our own behavior even a little, we create opportunities for more authentic encounters and enhanced relationships.

This third book is another build and targets my work with executive transformation in a group experience. Group coaching is a yearlong, facilitator-led encounter where the participants are challenged to learn and grow in a small cohort of leaders of similar experience with relatively like needs. The book's underlying focus is on how the coach can use and evolve the fundamentals of Jungian psychology—understanding Self and wholeness, the individuation process, complexes and shadow—with groups. It is a guide to raising the emotional intelligence of the individual participants through processing with others in homologous situations.

> "The privilege of a lifetime is to become who you truly are."
> C. G. JUNG

Much of my work centers on the growth and development of leaders. Like all of us, leaders are most effective when they start with knowing themselves and gaining insights to the psyche and evolving Self. When we see how we're maintaining the psychic structures of our personality, we can determine when it's time to make new choices. When we're conscious of how those structures get in the way and use up our energy, we become more agile and able to self-manage more efficiently. Then we begin to see how to manage others more effectively. When you enable groups to see the world from a more conscious lens, they can have an impact on developing a culture that is less blaming and shaming and more encouraging and innovative. These are the efforts that truly enable increased employee satisfaction and engagement.

There are also challenges inherent in the process for both coaches and group participants. As each member undertakes many experiments and shares those experiences, they rub up against their likenesses and differences in the group, igniting emotions, resonant ahas, and the pain of old wounds. They experience their power, or lack thereof. If it's true that we adapt who we are depending on who we're relating to and multiply that by 10, it gets very messy very quickly.

Jung read a great range of works and drew on them for his understanding of the human condition. When he discovered Dante Alighieri's *Comedia* (1320), he found it highly revealing as a metaphor for the individuation process—that journey of finding the true Self. Dante uses the Italian phrase, *mi ritrovai,* to express the idea of "recovering myself."[2] In the group work, a transformational effort, the individual is attempting to do just this—to re-find or recover the Self. And like with the journey of the main character in the story (poem), participants might find themselves going through a bit of hell or experiencing some new awareness of some difficulties they've been through in the past. Transformational growth is more of a spiraling pathway than a linear progression. We reexperience ourselves at different stages of life on the archetypal journey.

The Insight Group Coaching Process, which I will describe in these pages, has evolved over many years and through my experiences in a variety of group process initiatives. But it has been my work with Jungian psychology that has enabled me to bring it together in a deeper, more meaningful way. The positive outcomes have inspired me to want to share this work with you.

Working with groups has been a compelling practice for me. It provides a great opportunity for the coach's own experiential learning, insight, and transformation. Indeed, inculcated in these pages you will find *my* transformational experiences. In journeying on this path to Self with group members, I have been able to refresh, renew, and more fully redeem my own soul. On many days I find I am the archetypal *water bearer*—providing drink to those parched on the journey. And, so often, the mutuality of the work has helped me with my own dehydration. It is my hope that you will have your own transformational experience as

---

2   David Whyte introduced me to this idea in a talk on a *Walking Tour* in Ireland.

you let yourself down into the deep waters of this work through reliving your own experiences and journaling about them. It requires curiosity and taking a certain level of interest in yourself. I leave you at the end of each chapter with some questions to propel you in that direction.

Foreword

I am delighted to write this foreword to Dr. Janet Steinwedel's latest iteration of her deeply creative way of envisioning leadership. It is her third volume, now forming a trilogy in the *Steinwedel Red Book Series.* May there be a fourth? We can only hope.

As a mythologist and teacher of literary classics from a Jungian perspective, I sense that Janet's vision of leadership is mythic in the way that Joseph Campbell developed the hero's journey from a mythically-inflected point of view. Her work is visionary in many ways, not the least of which is placing us, the reader and participant in her workshops, squarely in the archetype of the quest. Questioning rather than asserting is her methodology, or if I may strain the language a bit, her *mythodology.*

Moreover, her work in each chapter, accompanied at the end with deeply reflective questions to ponder in the individual reader-participant's own life, has the feel of a mythic exploration to open up some of the perhaps undiscovered terms of their own quest. And, accompanying this rich structure is a range of deeply provocative quotes placed judiciously in each of the chapters to evoke further reflection. Here is one of many favorites of mine that I copied into my journal to reflect on repeatedly. It is C.G. Jung reflecting on the word *vocation:* "One must obey his own law as if it were a daemon whispering to him of new and wonderful paths. Anyone with a vocation hears the voice of the inner man: he is *called.*" Janet's own calling to this work and, as Campbell suggests, heeding the call, then submitting to it because it is greater than the one being called, seems to me to be the bedrock of her research, her guidance and most importantly, her attitude towards those who are fortunate to become her students.

I say this because Janet implicitly reveals throughout her work that leadership emphasizes so much more of the person than does management. As I read each chapter and pondered the questions she posed in the spirit of encouraging her participants to become students of their own complex psyches, I sensed that management's ethos derives more from an ego perspective, while leadership is an archetypal image whose origin is soul-based. Janet emphasizes throughout this volume how becoming conscious is itself key to leading, not just in one's work but in leading an authentic life. Her refusal to separate one's work from one's ontological presence in the world is one of the book's greatest strengths. To use one of her own rich images, she sees herself as an "archetypal water-bearer," a nourisher and refresher of the soul. I would offer that her angle of vision on both leading and teaching is *mythopoetic;* by that I mean that she herself, in concert with her participants, are shaping or reshaping their own personal mythologies to better place themselves in accord with the world in all of its dimensions, not just their occupations. Such a rich enterprise that strives to reach into as many dimensions of their lives as possible, involves a striving for a coherent life, one that is conscious of soul and the enriching qualities that such a quest can promote.

To achieve successfully what I have just pointed to above, Janet's quest includes as well exploring each individual's alignment with their values, to question where an individual is at odds with their own myth and to engage a reflective remembering to help them with becoming more in accord with their true selves. This is indeed soul-making at its most rich and evocative. Its progress includes bringing into consciousness so many of Jung's elements in his psychology that Janet outlines: the Self, wholeness, the process of individuation, complexes, shadow recognition and many others.

In this regard, I enjoyed her courage in naming and describing particularly challenging situations and individuals in class where she accepted the conflict and thought through on the spot how best to apply her way of seeing each individual to the current uncomfortable but not insurmountable series of events. In the process she revealed to those present her courage in allowing her own vulnerability to be present. In my decades in the classroom I know what it can require for the teacher to show where s/he is most human and working from that position.

I end this short foreword by applauding her as well for her deep belief in the value of journaling: "I find reflective writing to be one of the most important aspects of transformational work." Here and elsewhere I found many common shared values with Janet in our love of teaching. Reading her work was like visiting an old friend, where she shared stories about what works with learners and what might be improved upon. Truly a gift to us are all three volumes on leadership. This capstone volume, so to speak, is a compilation of wisdom earned and discovered through decades of leadership coaching. I count myself fortunate to be one of her students.

Dennis Patrick Slattery, Ph.D.

Emeritus Faculty, Mythological Studies Program at Pacifica Graduate Institute

Author of *Riting Myth, Mythic Writing: Plotting Your Personal Story*

Part I

Learning About Group Process

"The individual has always had to struggle to keep from being overwhelmed by the tribe. If you try it, you will be lonely often, and sometimes frightened. But no price is too high to pay for the privilege of owning yourself."

FRIEDRICH NIETZSCHE

I

What Is Group Process and How Does It Benefit Leadership Development?

"Just as total societies develop a culture, social structure, laws, and traditions as a way of stabilizing themselves, so organizations must find ways to conserve and stabilize their culture and structure."

EDGAR SCHEIN

Over the last 25 years, a lot has changed in Leadership Development, especially in the ways in which programs are designed and delivered. Unlike the days when a single trainer led exercises over a three- to five-day period, there are few programs today that are merely facilitator-led and fewer that meet for multiple days in a row. In the last five years, there has been a string of articles (from *Harvard Business Review*, LinkedIn, and some of the largest human capital consulting firms) expressing a need to drastically change how we do leader development in organizations. It is fair to say that companies can no longer expect people to be engaged in learning because they tell them to be. It is not a "build it and they will come experience." The right information, aligned with corporate strategy, offered at the right time because it is relevant to the work and goals of the individual, and with their schedule taken into consideration, will likely win the day. Of course, it must incorporate some mix of classroom time, collaborative assignments, assessment and coaching, e-learning, and consideration of global issues and context. A tall order.

The roots of this conversation about the value of leadership development programs may have started with the "War for Talent." I was very much involved with such an effort in the Financial Services firm where I was an internal leader of Training and Organizational Development over 20 years ago. We were anticipating a shortage of talent by 2020, along with increased competition internationally and domestically, and knew we had to learn how to make better decisions about hiring, promoting, and developing our leaders. [See example: Table 1: Korn Ferry Ad, 2/2019]

Table 1

More and more observers agree that a talent scarcity is looming—and that this shortage will make finding and keeping the right people with the right skills increasingly challenging for organizations.

Organizations need to re-think their employee development if they are looking to find answers to this issue:

- Only 37% of organizations understand their current skills gaps[1].
- 94% of employees say that they would stay longer at a company if it invested in their career development[2].

If you want to get ahead of the competition in the talent crunch, it's time to take a different look at your employee development.

That effort birthed what came to be called Talent Management and made for significant improvement in our succession planning processes. Now many organizations systematically look at the breadth and depth of their talent and assess their readiness for promotional opportunities. There is more consideration for how individuals can bring the best of themselves to the efforts of meeting organizational goals. Competencies are drawn up expressing what it will take for leaders to be successful in that particular organization at this time in its life cycle. There is regular strategizing on how to more effectively engage employees. The C-suite collaborates with its leadership development colleagues (internal and/or external) on the design and investment in projects and rapid experiments that will both challenge and be instructive, calling for iterative measures in an effort to be better and innovate faster.

Organizations are coming to understand that the old approach to Leadership Development is not working, and many are experimenting with varied methodologies that include alignment with current challenges, technology, and brief experiments. They're becoming more agile in an effort to hear and be responsive to their leader's most urgent concerns.

> "In our most recent research, we found that leadership development is the number one talent management function that needs the most improvement, as identified by 43% of companies."
>
> JOSH BERSIN, DELOITTE

Among them is the reality that today's employees want challenging *and* meaningful work, and many managers don't know how to begin to meet their aspirations. They often don't have the time or the skills for thoughtful development conversations. Their project teams are scattered across countries and continents, adding to the need for more conscious and courageous communication. They need better "soft skills." Most leaders will not ask for emotional intelligence training, but it is the very thing that will enable the growth and maturity many organizations seek. They need to take a pause now and again to consciously build relationships and develop their thinking. They must enhance their agility and resourcefulness. But, *how*, you might ask? How can you do this when so much is continuously changing? How do you refuel in flight?

We know from the work of Malcolm Knowles that adults learn best when they are internally *motivated* to learn and they feel there's an *immediate relevance* to learning. As noted, few leaders have the time or patience to sit in daylong, never mind multiple-day training sessions that don't focus on or incorporate what the participant sees as relevant. They are eager to get to the *real* work. Many "off-the-shelf" leadership programs are criticized for their inability to meet the varied needs, learning styles, and motivations of potential participants.

Executive coaching, a customized approach that focuses on what the leader needs right now, has grown exponentially over these last 20 years in an effort to plug the gap in leader development. And yet it is not cost effective for every leader to have a coach.

"I've looked at some training programs for leaders. I'm discouraged by how often they focus on the development of skills to manipulate the external world rather than the skills necessary to go inward and make the inner journey. I find that discouraging because it feeds a dangerous syndrome in leadership."

PARKER PALMER

Enter group coaching. My experience, heading up leadership development in organizations over many years, was that small-group work, managed well, had great potential. Over the last decade as an external coach and leadership development consultant, I have molded my ideas for effective group coaching into a model I refer to as "Insight Group Coaching." The IGC model includes eight to 10 participants and limited meeting time. It incorporates coaching from the facilitator and teaches the participants to provide each other with peer coaching. The loose-tight methodology enables changes in the plan in order to meet the most pressing needs of the group.

We already know the coaching model is a very effective one. Incorporating those skills with my group facilitator role strengthens my ability to utilize the knowledge and concerns of those in the room. Balancing support and challenge ensures compelling conversation and safety. Insights and new questions bring engagement and commitment to the work. We will delve into specifics of the Insight Group Coaching model in Part II.

Many of you have likely come out of the Organizational Development and Change Management fields and know a thing or two about group process. You've read Edgar Schein and know what it means to pay attention to what is happening between and to the group members. You've likely taken part in Human Interaction Labs for the experience of being part of a group and then analyzing what took place in the group and in yourself. You know about *holding the space* and *being a container*. You value witnessing or observing many less obvious behaviors taking place in the room. You're very skilled with Tuckman's five stages of group development: forming, storming, norming, performing and adjourning. These are foundational to the work. IGC brings these ideas and processes together with a modified leadership development design using the Analytical Framework (CAF model, see appendix) of my executive coaching work.

Questions to consider

Which of these ideas and processes are familiar to you? (Or, are there others?)

Why are you interested in group work?

What do you want to understand more thoroughly in order to prepare yourself to do group work?

_____

_____

_____

_____

_____

_____

_____

_____

_____

_____

_____

_____

_____

_____

_____

_____

_____

_____

_____

_____

_____

_____

_____

_____

_____

_____

II

A Review of Group Model Designs and Techniques

"We read the world wrong and
say that it deceives us."

RABINDRANATH TAGORE

In this chapter, I will introduce the many bits and pieces of what came to be the Insight Group Coaching model. This will both show you that it is an *evidence based[1]* process and provide an example of how people draw their experiences and insights into a comprehensive and meaningful approach to such work.

My first foray into understanding group process was through my Training and Organizational Development MS from St. Joseph's University in Philadelphia, which provided me opportunities to practice the skills noted in the first chapter. We had classes explaining the application of family systems theory, developing norms, considering types of groups, and leadership in groups, and then we applied it by working in groups in order to experience the various aspects of group interaction.

One of my favorite classes was on process consulting where we learned about creating trust and safety, and honed our skills in designing assessment processes and providing the diagnosis of an assessment. We learned early that "it is a key assumption underlying PC [process consultation]

---

1   An evidence-based approach links theory, research, practice, and results.

that the client must learn to see the problem for himself by sharing in the diagnostic process and be actively involved in generating a remedy" (Schein 1988). This in particular stuck with me and resonated in my future training as a coach and again as I designed the group coaching work.

Another key insight gained from my studies and reinforced through my experiences was that we all face some similar problems in joining a new group. Schein specified four key challenges: *Identity, Control & Influence, Needs & Goals,* and *Acceptance & Intimacy* (Schein 1988). These often involve hidden emotional issues that can create a fair amount of tension for the individual and the group, which the facilitator must be able to help resolve. I have come face-to-face with each of these challenges and have had to navigate through them. Had it not been for continuously doing my own emotional and psychological work, I could not have made use of these opportunities. And, I certainly would not have valued them from a deep enough place to support transformational experiences for my group members (and me).

Later work for my PhD took me into Gestalt training, Tavistock group experience and Jungian psychology, all adding key components to my understanding of effective group process. These approaches were more than tangential. Fritz Perls (the psychoanalyst who developed the Gestalt school into what it is today, often referred to as the Father of Gestalt Therapy) was a student of Freudian psychoanalysis but took his work in a similar direction to Jung (20 years his senior). Perls had a "phenomenological and subjective approach to therapy, noting that many of us split off experience (thoughts, sensations, emotions) that are uncomfortable" (Riga 1999-2017). While I had worked with some Gestalt ideas prior (e.g., cycle of awareness and figural vs. background, etc.), this was an intensive training that opened me to my biases and projections, making for a personal transformation. Growth in my own self-awareness and in the understanding of how important self-knowledge is for any real development was reinforced by Charlie Seashore[2], my professor at Fielding

---

2   Dr. Seashore held faculty positions at Fielding Graduate University, American University/ NTL Master's Program in Organization Development, the Washington School of Psychiatry, and Johns Hopkins University. He was an organizational consultant and coach for over 40 years in Washington, D.C., and served as president of the Lewin Center for Social Change, Action and Research.

Graduate University, through the very effective, intensive small-group experiences he introduced us to (e.g., T-groups, HI Labs).

A Tavistock group process weekend that I engaged in during the summer of 2000, while initially striking me as too regressive, was ultimately eye opening, giving me plenty to work with relative to the complexes working within me for a long time. In this process, the group is meant to become a mirror (and actually a group always has this capacity). It is a means of enabling us to see ourselves and provides an opportunity to discuss and observe different personal approaches ("ways of being") as they relate to boundaries, responsibilities and experiences. The methods are derived from the work of Wilfred Bion, a British psychoanalyst. His design focused on leadership and the relationship of authority (leadership) to the members of the group and within subgroups. He saw the collective entity as germane to understanding the individual.

The trained leaders of the group (six in my particular weekend, with 50-60 participants) followed a strict protocol over the three days in which we interacted in small and large groups. At the end, they provided feedback to certain individuals they were secretly observing.

The woman who I learned was watching my behaviors and taking notes on my contributions had a professional image and a somewhat hard disposition. When she saw me in the room with her other designees, she was quick to tell me I was in the wrong room. I confirmed that this was the room to which I was assigned. She asked my name and looked at her notes. She blushed with embarrassment and then acknowledged that indeed I was on her list and she did have notes for me. Then in the manner of a "Tavi" leader, she took responsibility for her emotional baggage and began to ask herself questions: Why didn't I recognize you? Why didn't I want to know you, to acknowledge you? She briefly answered her questions giving us the opportunity to see how this "mirror" works. She said, "Why would I want to give you any recognition? ... You're so well put together, every detail attended to, and you're confident as well." I was pretty shocked. Having had a first career in fashion merchandising, finishing it with a stint at Saks Fifth Avenue, I certainly did learn how to "put myself together." I'd been aesthetically minded for a long time. As I approached my 11th birthday, my mother signed me up for an etiquette course called "White Gloves and Party Manners." I took to it nicely. The store that sponsored the program asked me to model in its fashion shows. All of this was at the root of all of what I was trying to process in the moments I was being talked at in the debriefing room. I was conflicted with feelings of defensiveness and confusion. I felt both proud and suddenly insecure about that pride. I was defending against the rush of memories of other women who I felt had treated me badly over the years, while also wondering if I provoked the treatment. It was an emotional experience that challenged me to look more consciously at the pros and cons of choosing to be well put together.

Prior to these experiences with two well-known processes, I was involved with an impactful group process in the financial services organization I worked in for six years. The corporate head of Talent Management was collaborating with Dick Dooley of The Dooley Group Inc., who designed the Leadership Learning Forum (LLF[SM]). Dick provided training programs for facilitators of his group process. In those sessions, he focused on specific skills but also brought home several principles and beliefs, including: *If I'm not learning and growing how can I expect others to be*; *my faults are capable of dominating my contributions*; and, *the finer tuning is the most challenging*. That last one sums up the most important work of a coach—we must do the fine-tuning on ourselves, and it's not easy.

Dick had the advantage of running his groups when organizations were still setting up training programs with multiple-day sessions. We met nine times for two to three days at a time over a year period. Participants were leaders from several of the organization's businesses and locations in the U.S. and U.K. The Leadership Learning Forum model included guest speakers, prereading, presenting, and a myriad of interesting exercises and discussion formats. I was fortunate to be included in a group and to have the opportunity to facilitate and support parts of the process in other groups between 1997 and 2000. The leaders grew personally, professionally and as colleagues. I felt there were many strong aspects to the process, but by the time I started to design my own group work, I realized a fair amount of what Dick had been doing wouldn't work in the strained workplaces of the day. For example, we read 37 books and nine articles in my group. I have a hard time getting participants to read four books in a year. And, of course, being in leadership training for two to three days at a time is a very rare occurrence these days. What I took from the experience was the knowledge of what processes and activities provoked engagement. For example, reading had a lot of value for stimulating thinking, challenging paradigms, and encouraging meaningful discussion. Additionally, holding participants responsible for leading dialogue throughout the program gave them an active role that built their commitment.

I was highly influenced by Dick's personal dedication to learning and his expectation that all leaders needed to continue their learning and challenge their understanding of people and relationships and how work gets done.

The final process that informed my approach comes from the Arbinger Group and a book it published called *Leadership and Self-Deception*. I received my first training on the material from one of the core members in 1998 and took part in a telecourse in 2007 to refresh my understanding of the principles. The Arbinger Group presents its approach to unearthing self-deception in a fable format set in a fictitious organization. It is analogous to the process Arbinger facilitates with families, encouraging family members to see our tendency as human beings to "keep ourselves from understanding ourselves" (Warner 1997). Once we become conscious of how we betray our thoughts and go unconscious in an effort not to take responsibility, we see this pattern everywhere. The key is to abstain from the temptation to show everyone else the errors of their ways and to concentrate on seeing these deceptions in one's own behaviors. It is quite liberating and can eliminate a lot of unnecessary conflict in one's life. This has become a core book in the Insight Group Coaching process and a real gift to the development of self-awareness.

Ancient wisdom tells us "when the student is ready the teacher will appear." In groups where the participants are ready to learn, we find the teachings all around us in a variety of modalities. For the 100 years that we've been studying adult learning, we don't have one clear theory to work from. In addition to the practices highlighted above, I have also gleaned a lot from the work of William Bridges (e.g., Transitions: Endings, Neutral Zones and Beginnings), Robert Kegan and Lisa Lahey (how individuals and groups make meaning and the "Big Assumption"), Malcolm Knowles (Andragogy, Self-Directed Learning) and Jack Mezirow (Transformative Learning Theory). Designing several leadership development training programs in my days as an internal consultant and leading countless training sessions (off-the-shelf programs) also informed my way forward. It has been an iterative process and will continue to evolve to meet the changing needs of organizations and their leaders.

Jung said, "Learn your theories and then set them aside," and "Learn not from my ways, but your ways." My intention is not to teach you a methodology but to encourage you to develop your own from your many life experiences and from understanding learning at a deeper level.

Questions to consider

Which theorists, programs and processes have impacted you most?

(As the facilitator? As a participant? As a trainee of group facilitation?)

What drives you in your efforts with the work of adult learning?

_____

_____

_____

_____

_____

_____

_____

_____

_____

_____

_____

_____

_____

_____

_____

_____

_____

_____

_____

_____

_____

_____

III

The Student-Teacher Archetype

"Everything good is costly, and the development of the personality is one of the most costly of all things."

C. G. JUNG

Jung valued the study of opposites that archetypal ideas present. One such archetype is the *Student-Teacher*. That is, to be whole in our expression of learning we must live both sides—we must play the student and be eager to learn new things, and we must act the teacher and put that learning into a methodology that enables others to learn. This sensibility is at my essence. I don't know if it is learned or has always been a part of me—I suppose it is both nature and nurture. And I believe it is within us all; after all, it is *archetypal*. That being said, how it shows up in each person will depend on the individual and their development over time. Today it seems that the very nature of organizations and their evaluation processes has employees more apt to mentor, advise, and tell about what they know rather than act the student. Yet, there comes a point in an executive career when one needs to shift out of all knowing and into curiosity to encourage others to share what *they* think, know, and observe. And certainly, in the shift to innovative leadership that many organizations have made in the last five years, it is imperative to open to possibilities and bring multiple ideas into the open for enhancing decisions and direction. Binary thinking is limited and limiting, and the IGC group process encourages everyone to think bigger and broader.

"The archetype is essentially an unconscious content that is altered by becoming conscious and by being perceived, and it takes its colour from the individual consciousness in which it happens to appear."

C. G. JUNG (9A, PARA 6)

This archetypal message is also important for the facilitator of group work. If there is no eagerness to learn from the experiences of the group members, there will be little discussion and few attempts to string together new ways of thinking. This work is a process of curiosity and discovery.

Insights on this archetype's relevance have been instructive in my setup of the group, letting participants know early in the process that there are no A's to be achieved and few rights and wrongs to adhere to. There is no report back to managers as to the value of an individual and his or her thinking. The expectation is that everyone is practicing expanded ways of leading. There's meant to be a certain liberation from the typical sense that one must demonstrate as much competence as possible.

Chris Argyris, a Harvard professor, taught a technique for mutual learning that requires balancing *advocacy* and *inquiry*. The teacher and student need to use both to be at their best and to gain the most value from an experience. In Argyris's model, it is equally important to be able to advocate a position or an idea as to be curious and ask good questions; to be prepared to listen and integrate the new thinking with other ideas already on the table. This promotion of collaborative learning encourages teacher and student to use both skills. It is a growing skill set and a highly ranked competency for leaders.

Now that you have some sense of what is at the root of the Insight Group Coaching model let's dig deeper into the guiding principles, specific elements, and coaching framework.

Questions to consider

Are you more teacher or more student? How do you know?

What goals will you set for bringing more attention to the Student-Teacher archetype in your life?

_____

_____

_____

_____

_____

_____

_____

_____

_____

_____

_____

_____

_____

_____

_____

_____

_____

_____

_____

_____

_____

_____

_____

Part II

The Insight
Group Coaching Model

---

*"Between stimulus and response there is a space.
In that space is our power to choose our response. In our
response lies our growth and our freedom."*

VIKTOR FRANKL

Introduction

As presented in the previous chapter, many roads led to my development of the Insight Group Coaching Model. In the same way, you will likely take varied paths based on your own background to this work of developing individuals in the group setting. Paying attention to your insights and transformative moments will bring you to a design and approach that is authentically yours. It is not the theories themselves but the meaning and clarity derived from them that are of value. As Marianne Schneider Corey and Gerald Corey warn in their book *Groups: Process and Practice*, if you operate in a theoretical vacuum, you will likely not be productive, but "[T]heory is not a rigid set of structures that prescribes, step by step, what and how you should function as a leader. Rather we see theory as a general framework that helps you make sense of the many facets of group process" (Schneider-Corey and Corey, 1997). Evolving the Insight Group Coaching Model has been enlightening and rewarding because it aligns with my values and it is meaningful to others. The Coreys note:

> Ultimately, the most meaningful perspective is one that is an extension of your values and personality. A theory is not something divorced from you as a person; it is an integral part of the person you are and an expression of your uniqueness (Schneider-Corey and Corey, 1997).

Know Thyself

Jung says, "There is no how of life, one just does it." That has been my experience, too. But when it comes to the how of leadership there are nearly as many schools of thought as there are people trying to become leaders. One message, however, always resounds. From the early Greek philosophers and even more ancient traditions right through our contemporary psychologists and philosophers, we hear the clear message of "know thyself."

Daniel Goleman, Richard Boyatzis, Peter Salovey, John Mayer, Joseph LeDoux and others who were at the forefront of the "Emotional Intelligence" movement that began some 30 years ago and continues in its importance, also adopted this principle of self-knowledge first. Coaches/group facilitators must do their work so they can be effective with, and good role models of self-awareness for, their groups. It has long been my belief that if participants in my group initiatives can move a notch up the scale of emotional intelligence, especially in their self-awareness and ability to manage what they learn about themselves, they will be much better at all of the managing and relating parts of their jobs. Many tell me they are better parents and partners because of the work as well.

"Try to be simple and always take the next step. You needn't see it in advance, but you can look back at it afterwards. There is no 'how' of life, one just does it…"

C.G. JUNG, LETTERS VOL. I, 10 JUNE 1950

You are likely familiar with the Myers Briggs Type Indicator (MBTI®) as a means of "knowing thyself." The initial purpose of the tool, designed by a mother-daughter team, was to help soldiers returning from World War II learn about their personalities in hopes of finding a job that would be suitable to them. Myers and Briggs built the tool from Jung's work on psychological types (see his book by the same name). The premise revolves around the unconscious drive toward *individuation*, or the individual's search for the fulfillment of his or her unique destiny. It is an effort that would culminate in wholeness if we could ever actually reach that point. Carl Jung did not see this work occurring in isolation but believed that it came through our desire for connection and relationship with like-minded others, in what he referred to as "kinship libido" (Hecht 2011). For Jung, libido is elevated to a much more robust idea than Freud's notion of unconscious sexual energy and aggression. Jung referred to it as the "broad motivating force animating all human endeavor" (Hecht 2011). Kinship libido, which drives our desire to be in all relationships, not just love (eros) relationships, is what we want to tap into if we want to see people make transformational growth. This understanding is of value for both the facilitator and the participants.

Group Think refers to a situation when individuals in a group come to think alike and have the same opinions, which escalates into an unhealthy inflation. With *Insight Group Coaching,* we're attempting to work against that—to differentiate and more clearly see how all participants' values, needs, personality styles, and interests unearth their unique personhood. It's generally an insight for people to realize that this uniqueness is a good thing. By the time I meet people for group work, they have often spent a lot of time trying to be connected to those who appear more powerful or successful, or to fit in with some in-crowd. So, the chance to be reinforced for being themselves is meaningful and positive, but an adjustment all the same. "Jung believed that significant psychic suffering resulted from trying to deny an inner process that called an individual to pursue ambitions that others did not understand or value" (Hecht 2011). And yet, early in our lives, we don't always trust that call from within. We get caught up with the energy of the collective and go about trying to be a success—whatever that means in our social environment. And, that's okay. As Jung said, "under no circumstances can individuation be the sole aim of psychological education. Before it can be taken as a goal, the educational aim of adaptation to the necessary minimum of collective norms must first be attained" (Jung 1971). For most, this minimum is obtained by the time one graduates from university. While to some degree we are continuously making small adjustments based on new communities we join, we are more ready, and appropriately so, every few years to take on additional attributes of a truly authentic position. If our maturity (i.e., self-awareness, reflection, resilience, empathy) is developing in tandem with our age and other forms of growth (e.g., technical, biological, moral), we integrate our uniqueness effectively. This is a necessity for bringing our optimal value to bear. Harvard Medical School professor and psychiatrist George Vaillant found in his research "that life stresses cause individuals to revert to less mature defensive strategies. By the same token, relationships with more mature persons help one move to higher adaptive levels" (Bentz 1989). Having a cohort to learn with enables greater opportunity for relationships with more mature individuals because they are all interested in working on such things and they're getting the tools to enhance how they do that.

Each Insight Group Coaching process starts with the coach/facilitator working with each participant separately to learn how each one is distinct and different from the group and to encourage this perspective seeking. In this role, I listen for intimations that they might be paying attention to some inner call or not yet ready to separate from the collective expectations. An upfront decision with Human Resources is a commitment of how many times the individuals will meet one-on-one with me. It is never less than three times and has been as often as every month for some contracts. I have included extra sessions for some individuals who just need a little more assistance in integrating the ideas or are working through a difficult time. This private time gives me an opportunity to see a bit behind the persona—the mask an individual wears to more comfortably meet and engage with others. Here I find a richer, more complex personality.

The value of gaining as much understanding of the participants upfront individually will be better understood as we dig into learning how the *Analytical Framework* aligns with group work. I'll be providing examples to better express the central parts of the model.

Questions to consider

What are some of the things you have learned about yourself as an adult?

How would you describe your leadership style?

Are you aware of a persona that you wear in order to engage with others with greater ease? Try to describe it (them) here.

I

Insight Group Coaching: Aligning the CAF Model with Group work

---

"But each technique carries a consistent message more important than any method—that each act that expresses trust in ourselves and belief in the validity of our own experience is always the right path to follow."

PETER BLOCK

If you've read book one or two of the *Red Book* series, you are familiar with the Coaching with an Analytical Framework, or *CAF*, model (see appendix). I have aligned the CAF model with Jung's framework for analysis. While there is some overlap, I am not suggesting that we provide analysis for our clients. I do think it is worth noting, however, that Jung's ideas of "confession," "elucidation," "education," and "transformation," have alignments with the conversations I am having relative to the four ways we engage, identified in the CAF model as "aspirations," "assessment," "coaching," and "transition" (AACT), in an effort to develop people beyond their current state of consciousness. It is also interesting to note that Jung wrote, "About a third of my cases are not suffering from any clinically definable neurosis, but from the sense-

"Even a happy life cannot be without a measure of darkness, and the word 'happy' would lose its meaning if it were not balanced by sadness. "

CG JUNG

lessness of their lives." Over and over again, I hear from clients that they want more meaning in their lives. They want to live more purposefully. There's a cacophony of voices addressing happiness, but being happy isn't so easy. And in the end, I'm not sure it would be enough. It's an idea worthy of provocation.

Aspirations

In my preparatory work with the HR executive (or other organizational sponsor) to design the plan for our 12-month process, I start the conversation the same way I do with my individual coaching, seeking to understand "aspirations." Just what is it that the organization wants leaders to *do, get* or *be* in a future state? To this end, I might start out asking: What is going particularly well with leaders in this organization? What are their strengths? The follow-up is, of course: What is not going well, where do your leaders tend to struggle? What are the aspirations for midlevel and more senior leadership? Typically, organizations have a set of leadership competencies and organizational values that help define what these things are, but they don't always match, which can be informative to both the HR leader and me. While I do want direction, I am not looking for hardline specifics that would diminish the opportunity to develop the individual strengths of each leader. For example, if I'm told, "We want every leader to delegate clearly every day what their subordinates should be doing and how they should be doing it," that would not be useful. Accomplishing this is not a promise I want to make. Do I want leaders to delegate well? Yes, but it is not the main mission of transformational initiatives. Additionally, how people will go about delegating will be different because *they* are different and each of their subordinates are different and if they develop strong relationships, the delegating will get done in the best form it can.

I also want to learn from the HR executive what each of the participants is known for. They are all high-potential or emerging talent, but there is usually some unconscious bias that is helpful to know. In other words, each has a "reputation." While it is important not to act on that reputation, it helps me in exploring where that reputation is coming from—good and bad.

This HR leader is, in turn, having a similar conversation with business leaders. It might go something like this:

> I am about to engage a coach to work with a group of eight-10 leaders across our businesses to enhance their leadership skills. If we take this on, what are the competencies and capabilities you would like to see more of in your leaders? What aspirations do you have for your leaders and what aspirations do you expect that they have for themselves? What kinds of development have you undertaken for your leaders in the last one to three years? What value has it had? What challenges are greatest for you at this time?

I talk with my contact about *my* aspirations for leaders in a general sense. I might say something like this:

> My experience is that leaders are often struggling with the ability to be collaborative and relational. I find that the *VUCA* (volatile, uncertain, complex, ambiguous) world we live in is straining leaders in one or more of those areas. I would like to see leaders have more of the capacity that enables them to achieve the resilience and capability to be skillful, effective, and fulfilled in their work.

> I often talk about the value in raising emotional intelligence through this process and that it is a transformational approach—an opportunity to develop one's maturity. I hope that participants will finish with more depth and enlargement and increased ability to adjust their ego position. If they can do this, they will be better at most things they do as leaders, not at just one or two skills they pick up along the way. My hope is that they'll be able to lead their employees in meaningful and generative ways. My mantra has been, *not change, but range.* I am not seeking to change the person, nor could I, but I can support an individual in gaining more range in their responses to challenging situations, "difficult" (or maybe just different) people, and changing environments. If they can become more agile and more open, they will find more success.

"While many features of the ego clearly do develop and change, particularly with regard to cognition, self-knowledge, psychosocial identity, competence, etc., one also senses an important continuity at the heart of the ego."

MURRAY STEIN,
MAP OF THE SOUL

Once a group has been chosen, I begin to have the aspiration conversation with each participant. Having some understanding of their hopes, dreams, and goals is key to my successful support of them. Jung's idea of "confession" is aligned and significant as this is when individuals divulge their frustrations, desires, and concerns, and test the level of trust between themselves and the analyst. In both situations, there is often some *catharsis* from just this act of sharing what they are truly feeling about their role, their level of success and their fears relative to the future they aspire to. I am listening for both their "confessions" and their inspirations. Do they feel they have a purpose, a path? Do they feel a calling? What got them to where they are today?

Assessment

The aspirational conversation I have with HR comes first, and I usually have the aspirational discussion with the participant in tandem with the assessment feedback. I adjust the assessments I use based on preferences of the client organization but most often I am using the MBTI® (Myers Briggs Type Indicator which reports personality preferences) and the Golden VAL® (Values Arrangement List, reporting operational and life values). These are always rich conversations where I learn a lot about the individual's perception of him- or her-self, their level of self-awareness, and their openness to greater insight and personal reflection.

While it is important not to see the data as complete truth and not to project expectations related to the assessments onto the client, the information does shorten the time needed to have relevant conversations about the participant's personality, style, values, and behavior.

Jung's idea of *elucidation* relates to bringing light to unconscious contents of the psyche. It is very hard to make what is unconscious conscious. Looking for complexes, neurosis and psychosis truly is the work of analysis.

My take is more focused on noticing that which is *subconscious*: ideas and paradoxes that are not readily available to the person, likely because the person chooses not to see them, or hasn't been challenged to see them. These are aspects of the psyche. We refer to it as shadow material, much of which is completely unconscious. We each have a shadow and we are not trying to eliminate that but to see these aspects of the personality for what they are and how they can help us. Murray Stein notes that "the ego is usually quite unaware that it even casts a shadow" (Stein 1998). He notes "that these are traits or qualities that have been suppressed because of cognitive or emotional dissonance…." and that the "contents of the shadow may change, depending upon the ego's attitudes and its degree of defensiveness" (Stein 1998). Not knowing of our shadow material limits our effectiveness and ability to be authentic. For example, I learned that one participant lost a sister early in her life and she felt some responsibility for that but had a hard time dealing with it because it was old news, was not relevant to her work life, and was not a socially acceptable conversation topic. But it was lodged in between her positive and negative self-concept, causing a sense of unworthiness. The average person is not going to go to therapy for this issue, and yet it can unconsciously get in the way of "success" as a mature individual.

Through the combined discussion of aspirations and assessment data, I get many clues as to where an individual is on his or her journey. I learn where the participants are probably free and where they are likely stuck. I can sometimes see complexes at work or begin to see certain aspects of their life that are split off. Here are two examples that will shed greater light on this work.

I was meeting with a 50-year-old woman who felt she had to take a call from her mother about 20 minutes into our conversation. She explained that she usually doesn't call during the workday and she was concerned. No problem, I thought that was reasonable. But after the call, she went on to explain that her mother is rather needy, and she's made a routine of calling her on her way to and from work. She added that she doesn't really mind, but sometimes it becomes burdensome. It seemed that if she doesn't initiate calls in turn, her mother worries and then begins to get "unreasonable." Since my coachee was an ESFJ (MBTI® meaning

"Extraverted," "Sensing," "Feeling" and "Judging") I could start with the assumption that she had a tendency for loyalty and helpfulness. In taking a quick glance at her prioritized values list (Golden VAL®) I noticed that *honesty, autonomy* and *accountability* were important operational values. But in service to what, I thought as I looked to the longer-term, life values. There I noted that *family* fell to the middle, *self-worth* was high along with *freedom* and *achievement*. That moved us into a conversation about how her values explained her situation with her mother. She hesitated and haltingly attempted an explanation before blurting out, "Well, they don't, and that's why I'm always stressed out, I guess." That enabled us to have a meaningful conversation (with several more to come) about how to be aligned with her values and meet her expectations for herself. And, as you might guess, our discussion went beyond her relationship with her mother, to the relationship she had with her boss and several of her direct reports.

In another situation, during an assessment feedback session with a young man of about 28 who was recently married and had a close bond with his 6-year-old daughter from a former college relationship, I noticed a general irritation or unsettledness about him. He was eager to get his information and get on with his day. But when we started to go through this INTJ's ("Introverted," "Intuitive," "Thinking," "Judging") values something appeared off. *Forgiveness, affection* and *tolerance* were among his core operational values, and *accountability* was number one. *Achievement* was the highest of his life values followed by *equality, self-worth, power* and *spirituality*. He started to say that these values were wrong, as if I'd mixed up the responses or brought him the wrong lists. Then it dawned on him that he didn't really feel right about the Type® description. As we went back over it he claimed that he was really a "Feeling" Type® but all of his role models were *Thinking* Types® and he'd been forcing himself into that mold. Interestingly, he was quite mature for his age, and we quickly

"We should know what our convictions are, and stand for them. Upon one's own philosophy, conscious or unconscious, depends one's ultimate interpretation of the facts. Therefore, it is wise to be as clear as possible about one's subjective principles. As the man is, so will be his ultimate truth."

C. G. JUNG

made a lot of progress after he achieved this new level of self-awareness. Within six months, he was moving quite differently in his world and had made adjustments to focus more of his efforts on what fulfilled him. Note that it wasn't that he couldn't or shouldn't do INTJ-style activities or behaviors but that it was wearing him out. With this new sense of himself, he could integrate the two styles thoughtfully and did it uncommonly well.

Coaching

For me, coaching is both a "Thinking" and "Feeling" activity managed through a reflective lens. It is a partnership that fosters creativity, authenticity, and effectiveness. Effectiveness will be determined by the goals set by the organization as well as the individual. Our outcomes are a product of both support and challenge. Providing support and challenge to an individual is one thing, providing it to a group is quite another. It cannot be focused on intellectualizing and understanding, as was the case with the majority of participants' education up till now. I am asking them to *feel* what is happening inside themselves. My getting to know the individuals prior to our first group session and working with their assessments gives me an opportunity to begin building trust and connection. This creates the intimacy that allows me to have some idea of how to approach and respond to a person in the group. With some understanding of each person—what they know, how they're experienced by others, and how they feel about their situation—I am much more able to facilitate skillfully. Insight to the following questions enables me to be more prepared: Individually and as a group are they more defended or more open and naturally trusting? Are they reserved or more affable? Did they appear to be excited about this opportunity or feeling it burdensome? Do they generally like their organization, their boss, the leadership? Do they know the other participants? Are they comfortable with me or seemingly skeptical?

Engaging the Group Thoughtfully

In the group, I tend not to bring in what I know about individuals unless they offer that up—and still I tend to be a bit cautious. I encourage people to step up but not necessarily *lean in*, meaning that I want them to engage and find ways to participate but I don't want them to feel pressured to be something they are not. I don't want them to put themselves in too risky a position too early in the process. Speaking up just to look appropriately assertive can be senseless. And yet, most interactions can be made useful to the group's (and the individual's) learning. For example, in one group I worked with, a young man spoke up easily and often. He seemed quite sure of himself and his understanding of leadership. The group generally seemed impressed that he had answers for nearly all situations. Since I couldn't stop him without embarrassing him, I tried to get others to give their perspectives by offering options, e.g.: Do you think what Tom was saying would work for you—why or why not? He soon came to see that this was not meant to be a solo act and in fact there were varying perspectives. This is an opportunity for Jung's ideas of *confession* and *elucidation* to play out in the group. And my opportunity to be sure I'm *educating* (the third phase of Jung's model) as well as challenging and encouraging. This is how to make use of situations that can feel awkward or even inappropriate. The idea is that there will always be what feel like errors in judgment but they can also be our best teachers. If no one in the group is ever "inappropriate," if there is too much care taken to be perfect, little to no learning will take place.

Mindful of creating a safe space and encouraging vulnerability, I begin by using a lot of plural pronouns in the monthly sessions, we, us, they, them. I refer to "leaders" at large and the challenges of organizational life. As the participants feel more comfortable, they speak up and own these characteristics, feelings, and behaviors. Then, in our following one-to-one sessions I can encourage more of that while supporting their confidence to speak up and share something of value when they get back to the group.

> "Do you know the tragedy I see in our institutions when leaders operate with a deep, unexamined insecurity about their own identity? These leaders create institutional settings which deprive *other* people of their identity as a way of dealing with the unexamined fears in the leaders themselves."
>
> PARKER PALMER

Paying attention to each individual's development process through, or in spite of, the collective energy is challenging. There can be a lot of noise to contend with. If we (group members play a role in this as they begin to assert norms for the group to follow) can manage the noise without discouraging participation and contrary views, there is value to be gained. It is my job to gather the salient factors that have been raised and present them through a question or a challenge with the intention that someone will share a small insight or a truly transformational moment. In one particularly "Extraverted" "Feeling" group, where the noise level was high and opinions were passionately expressed, I decided to stop the group and asked the participants to pull out their journals to quietly answer some questions. I chose questions based on our conversation that morning to get at their "Introverted" "Thinking" and bring some objectivity and logic (e.g.: What happens when an organization goes through change? What are the two most challenging aspects of the culture for the organization right now?). I then moved to some "Introverted" "Feeling" questions to bring their subjective spirit into play (e.g.: What good and bad is happening to you in this time of great organizational change? What are you noticing, good and bad, that is happening to your team? What do you want to do to bring more harmony and joy to you and your team?). Then I asked them to offer one thought or feeling to the group if they wished to. I made notes to bring into the next one-on-one coaching sessions.

The coach/facilitator's job is to make the group safe, but not so safe that nothing happens. The participants are often waiting for me to set the challenge. When I do, there is almost always someone ready to step in and respond: After all, these are emerging and high potential leaders—they are not typically shy. In the check-in round of one group's sixth meeting, a woman courageously noted that she was feeling less confident now than she did at the start. That could sound terrible, except that I recognized it as the beginning of transformation, and it provided grist for a great conversation mill. Less confidence means not being certain, which might mean you're considering other perspectives, approaches, possibilities outside of what you have "known." We are looking for growth and enlargement, for more depth and breadth. We need the wiggle room of uncertainty in order to develop the agility to shift the ego position as appropriate to the situation and so that growth can take place. Remember, the ego is the center of the conscious field, and when it is fearful, it wants to believe it knows everything and hold its ground; when it feels safe, it can explore what is unknown.

Another part of the "C," or, coaching aspect of our AACT/CAF model, is that group members must engage in *peer coaching* ("Insight Coaching"), with others in the group in between our monthly sessions. This enables them to share feelings, reinforce ideas and applications, experiment with models and processes, and think through various organizational meetings they want to plan for. You will find more information on peer coaching in the next chapter on the operational components of group work.

In order to encourage coaching conversations in the participants' relationships with their managers, I suggest that they update them with their insights and questions and get their perspective on at least one leadership issue that's on their mind. This usually doesn't happen until after the third group meeting (and after the second one-on-one with the coach/facilitator). I don't suggest these conversations too early, as participants don't really have a handle yet on what is taking place and what they actually want from this transformational opportunity. In fact, I try to persuade my HR contact (and or the sponsor) before we get started to hold off the managers in the early months from asking questions like, "How do you like the program so far?" Growth and transformation are difficult. It isn't always something you "like." There can be times when you feel downright incompetent. So, it is helpful when individuals partaking in the process can start the conversation on their own terms. I often give them tips on how to guide the conversation they want to have with their boss.

> "The first half of life is devoted to building a healthy ego. The second half is going inward and letting go of it."
>
> C. G. Jung

In one instance, a group member went to both HR and the sponsor to make a complaint about me. She had misunderstood a challenge I made to her to think about some behaviors as a direct criticism. I thought she was further along in her development and had no sense that I was putting her in distress. Fortunately, I had had a good conversation with my HR contact about early discomfort with the process—although I had never experienced this kind of response before—and she handled the situation very well with the sponsor and with me (see box with HR leader's experience). It was the one time I really thought I had blown it. I learned a lot from the experience, having spent a lot of hours reflecting on what happened. Fortunately, the participant also learned a lot, and we parted with a strong relationship intact.

HR Leader's Experience:

When the group member brought her concerns to my attention, I tried to listen to understand what might be causing what seemed to be a strong and defensive reaction. I had enough confidence in the process and the coach to know I needed to dig under the initial feedback to really understand the situation. I know this kind of personal change can be hard. It can make people feel vulnerable. In this situation, it seemed to me that this vulnerability led the participant to become defensive about the process and the coach. After hearing her concerns, I reminded the participant about what this group coaching opportunity was about and the possible benefits. While the participant came around and ultimately stayed with it, and, I believe, feels she made strong progress; I was reminded that these types of groups are often microcosms of 'the real world'. There was a real growth opportunity for this participant to think about the feedback, her reaction to that feedback and how that same reaction may show up in daily work and life. This was a unique opportunity for the participant to experience the feedback in a safe, development-focused setting. That is a gift.

Transition

By the time we reach the ninth meeting, which is the final meeting except for a "check-in" session three months later (the one-year point), the group is well connected and feeling quite comfortable with one another and the group leader. These are the last opportunities to pave the way for a smooth transition from the safety net of the group and the coach to resources in the organization to which they feel a good level of confidence for discussing future issues and concerns. They know their go-to people for certain kinds of support and they have mostly secured better partnerships with their bosses. Some have mentors in place. They commit to staying in touch with members of the group. On occasion, someone going into a new role or having a big challenge to manage will contract with me for some extra one-to -one sessions.

Upon completion of the group, most participants have progressed through some growth stages that would fall into the "transforma-tional" realm (as per Jung's model) not unlike the stages of the analytical engagement: "encounter, revelation, intimacy, interpene-tration, combination, death of limited personal consciousness, and emergence of more whole, authentic consciousness." (Hecht 2011) You likely recognize the use of many of these or similar terms from the discussions above, but let's revisit them briefly.

- **Encounter:** This period is the meeting up initially of two individuals—each participant with me, their coach; then, the group and me; and finally, the individuals with each other. Encounter involves connection, listening, and mutual learning. For the coach/facilitator, it includes answering questions, directing the way forward, and building trust and rapport.

- **Revelation:** You have heard me refer to "insight," which is in fact equivalent to revelation. The coach/facilitator is trying to stir up opportunities for revelation, first in the initial one-on-one conversation and assessment feedback session; then, in subsequent individual coaching sessions, and in the group coaching sessions through the assignments, journal prompts, and discussions. Sometimes things are being revealed to the participants and sometimes they are revealing their insights to me in a "confession"-like interaction.

- **Intimacy:** There is a requisite closeness, a necessary rapport, to enable one to see and discuss their strengths and weaknesses, the errors of the past, and the shadow aspects of their personality. Without intimacy there is no vulnerability, and without vulnerability there can be no real learning.

- **Interpenetration:** This is the psychological term referring to the desired experience of each person in the group (to some degree), including the coach/facilitator, of mutual penetration—you've affected me, and I've affected you. When we talk about projection, transference and countertransference (mostly in book #2), we are referring to how interpenetration is stimulated. You've gotten to me in a way that has changed me.

- **Combination:** Using the MBTI®, which draws on Jung's work in "Psychological Types," enables the participants and me to learn about their combination of Typology. For example, when I refer to the "Introverted Thinking" Types or "Extraverted Feeling" Types, I am referring to Jung's combinations. I also consider the combination of the group Type and my Type for further information on how we might be challenged or fall into a false understanding of each other.

- **Death of limited personal consciousness:** This is a particularly important aspect of my philosophy. It is what I mean when I speak of the growth and enlargement, the moving up a level in one's emotional intelligence and the increasing authentic leadership that happens over time. We generally hear a bit about these deeper experiences in the participant's final, individual presentation to the group. This is a three- to five-minute explanation of insights, growth, and next steps. Many comments have been previously made in some form or another along the way, but there are always some new confessions, new disclosures, and interesting proclamations. It is a time of celebrating their experiences and new level of resilience.

- **Emergence of more whole authentic consciousness:** This is characterized by the development of personal authority, and clarity on "who I really am" and "what I really believe."

Questions to consider

What are some of your experiences of transformational learning?

Where have you experienced your own growth and enlargement?

Note an example of your own authenticity coming to light.

_____

_____

_____

_____

_____

_____

_____

_____

_____

_____

_____

_____

_____

_____

_____

_____

_____

_____

_____

_____

_____

_____

_____

_____

_____

_____

_____

II

Operational Components of Group Coaching

"When you have disciplined people, you don't need hierarchy. When you have disciplined thought, you don't need bureaucracy. When you have disciplined action you don't need excessive controls. When you combine a culture of discipline with an ethic of entrepreneurship, you get the magical alchemy of great performance."

JIM COLLINS, *GOOD TO GREAT*

Stepping away from the CAF model and Jungian psychology, let's consider the nuts and bolts of what is operationally necessary to run a group.

Creating a Schedule and Determining Location

Once a contract has been made with the HR leader, I sketch out a yearlong schedule (10 meetings) of reading, peer coaching, presenting, journaling, and all the other aspects that enable the group to operate efficiently yet meaningfully. I refer to it as a loose-tight approach as it provides a guide, but it is flexible. (A rules-oriented approach is inadequate for transformation, as I explain later.) If a discussion goes longer than the time I've allotted and the group feels it's important, then we adjust. If a book that participants are reading doesn't feel like a good fit, we can abandon it and replace it with another. The process becomes co-owned and, in this way, ensures engagement and commitment from the participants. And yet, it is not a free-for-all; there is a leader for a reason, and we do have to accomplish certain objectives. Part of the reason for a skilled practitioner is to understand the value of aspects that the attendees cannot yet appreciate and see them through.

In one situation, a woman spoke up in the third meeting, telling me very directly that I was giving the members too much work. They couldn't read all of what I had assigned. She secured her comments by noting, "and I've talked with others, and they agree." My leadership and curriculum design expertise were being openly challenged, and I had to make a very quick decision about how I would respond. I tried to separate out the personal from the objective concerns. I decided to go back to my expectations of them and take it away from me. In order to manage this transference and countertransference I told them that I could appreciate that each would feel the burden of the extra work at times and assured them that if they were *all* feeling a strain that they did need to let me know. However, I also told them that they needed to get away from a university mindset. I reminded them that there was no "A" to get in this process. I would not test for what they read or did not read. It was their responsibility to be ready for a robust conversation in our meetings. I lightened the atmosphere by bringing it back to the complainer's Type® and noting, that of course she would be trying to read every word on every page and that that wasn't necessary, but a personal choice. We all laughed and moved on. In this way, I hoped to convey to her a lighthearted message as well about potential rigidity.

The group is aware that the competencies and the overarching goals for our process are determined by the organization's leadership and are not arbitrarily chosen by me. If, for some reason, some element brings contention, we can discuss that with the sponsor or HR contact. But this is a rarity. In most cases, this will tell you more about the individual than about the design. It is important to have your antennae up for frustration and concerns. In the example above, the group members got it right away and took responsibility for themselves. The individual was a bit annoyed, but with a few other interactions over the months she also gained some important insight.

When I first started group work, we always met in one location. But as global organizations wanted to include leaders from other countries, we tested out videoconferencing. Because their systems are top-notch, we don't deal with delays in the audio, and it runs very smoothly. I am quite adamant that these cannot be teleconference meetings. Calling in is a disruption for those in attendance. It breaks the feeling of safety and real connection, and the person calling in is generally multitasking, which is not at all conducive to transformational learning. At times I will travel to other locations to facilitate a session in order to meet in person with more of the group members. We also encourage members to schedule travel so that they are in locations with at least one other participant rather than by themselves in a conference room. In one situation, all the members came into the headquarters office for one monthly meeting so they could all be together. We extended our two-hour plan so they were able to get the most from their travel.

The Invitation

Each person is individually invited by the sponsor, HR, or by his or her boss. This gets decided by each organization relative to the culture and what it wants to achieve. The invitation should be special, to ensure that each individual feels good about being chosen for this initiative. In some situations, this includes an invitation from the president/CEO. In organizations that have supported multiple groups, a former participant might take part in this process. Whatever will make the invitation most authentic and valued is the general rule of thumb. In one organization, the sponsor (a senior level physician leader) and the Chief Human Resources Officer called each of the invitees personally to let them know of the honor to be chosen and the value they had received from being a part of the process themselves.

The 10 meeting dates are typically indicated on the invitation so they get plugged into calendars as soon as possible. Often an admin-

"We invite that presence through the sincere tone and warmth of our *Invitation*. When participants have received this kind of invitation there is a better chance that they will show up physically, and a much better chance that they will arrive with *presence*, ready to participate fully in the gathering."

CRAIG AND PATRICIA NEAL,
THE ART OF CONVENING

47

istrative assistant is aligned with the initiative. This individual then sends out calendar invitations with locations to make it very easy for the participants to get to the right place at the right time. They also reserve the room/s, order snacks, send out the books and materials, and assist with videoconferencing details. In my experience, they are a vital link to a well-run initiative.

Setting Expectations and Creating Norms

In the one-to-one with me prior to the first group session, along with providing assessment feedback, I begin to set the expectations for each participant. This includes the expectation that they will attend each and every session. We want all of the participants at every meeting because it changes the group when someone is missing, and the individual missing loses continuity with the group and the process. Of course, these are busy people with multiple meetings to attend and places to be. I emphasize that the difference is that this is truly for them, for their development, and for their future success.

Insight Group Coaching is not a program and not a methodical approach to learning, which makes it more difficult to explain. You really just have to experience it. That being said, many participants want to know what is expected of them. They want a syllabus, they want to do it "right," and they want to leave with an "A." I attempt to break them of that thinking in the first meeting. As noted, there are no "A's," no report cards back to their managers, not many "rights" and "wrongs," and their syllabus is intentionally incomplete. I reinforce that this is a process in motion, with blank spaces. It is flexible. It is not a classroom with definite goals for each session. That leeway is important for their freedom to think, play with ideas, and deal with what is most concerning in the moment. This is an opportunity to bear with the ambiguity and uncertainty of daily life in a way that enables them to build agility—to be improvisational while still being intentional. While initially this is difficult for some to accept, they do eventually get the value in my seeming madness. It is why my efforts to build trust with them from the very start are so important. One way I do that is to laugh with them at the absurdity of my request and to say, "I know this is going to sound crazy, but I'm going to ask you to trust me and to trust that there will be much to gain from the experience."

Confidentiality is important to the ethics. It is a necessary expectation. It's okay to talk about most ideas and issues outside the room but without naming names or spelling out specific situations. And if someone says, "It is important to me that this not be talked about outside this room," that request must be honored. It is the facilitator's job to hold the space for what is not yet clear or ready for prime time. Providing the safety that enables vulnerability is a must for transformational learning, and that includes respecting privacy. I want it to be clear that this is a place of experimentation and learning, not of knowing and stubbornly adhering to the way one has always done things or the way it "should" be done.

Introductions take place in the first meeting, and the participants seem to enjoy telling the others about their career progressions and current status. In one first meeting, I remember going right to the two-hour mark and realizing I hadn't introduced myself as they were rushing for their phones and the door. When we gathered at the next monthly session, I began by noting this and gave them a short overview of where I'd come from and how group coaching came to be. In less than a minute I could tell they didn't much care. I had been working in the organization long enough that I had a reputation (fortunately, a good one) and I think they just didn't need to know my credentials. We quickly moved on to their check-in. (Silently, and later out loud, I had to laugh at my relative unimportance. I was a tool for their learning.)

> "Ethics are not a collection of commandments and prohibitions to abide by, but a natural inner offering that can bring happiness and satisfaction to ourselves and others."
>
> DALAI LAMA

Checking in occurs at the beginning of every session. I want to hear about the month between meetings and what the participants have been thinking about, experimenting with, and discussing. I listen. I encourage connection to each participant's values and personality styles (e.g., I'll ask a question of the individual something like, "So that compulsion wouldn't have anything to do with your Type®, would it? Can you tell me the connection you see?"). I laugh with them and feel into their concerns, just enough to build rapport and model emotional intelligence. Check-ins are an alchemical process. They are the sharing of reactions and interactions that are occurring. The alchemist's goal was to turn base metals into gold, and those who understood it as a metaphor for psychological processes knew that referred to human growth. The check-in time is an opportunity to hear about how an individual struggled with an idea, implemented a new approach, saw something they didn't like in what they were doing, or in some other way began the process of seeing things anew, enlarging themselves, shifting their style, finding the gold in their personality or leadership. When they bring their insights to consciousness, they interact in the field and transform.

Peer Coaching

Each participant is paired with other members throughout the year. In this way, they have a debrief partner (*Insight Partner*) with whom to review ideas, models, and their latest insights or revelations. This activity helps them keep ideas alive between monthly meetings. They are encouraged to *inquire, reflect,* and *challenge* in these one-hour meetups (in person where possible, but sometimes it must be through videoconferencing. Phone calls are a last resort). They *inquire* as to what had impact, what they want to try to incorporate in their management or leadership style, and what is working for them so far. They may also *reflect* on their experiences and successes, but they should refrain from advising one another except in the case where one has special knowledge and the other wants to be educated on it. In many instances, they are paired across disciplines and functional departments and can get a better understanding of the larger system if they choose. This peer-to-peer learning and exchange are always noted as important benefits of the initiative. It is a new skill for most and a benefit that continues for many.

Once some rapport is built, they might start *challenging* one another to try something new—softly and in a nondemanding way. It is more of a suggestion based on what the peer coach heard the person say. If there is something in the comment that the partner finds useful, she might jump on it, discussing the resonance. If it touches a bit of a tender spot, she might just comment that it's interesting and she'll think about that. However, if the person is ready, she will often bring the experience to the check-in to share with the larger group in the monthly meeting.

The Insight Partners stay together for two to three months and then move on to a new partner. As the coach, I make the pairings and put people together in partnerships that I believe will support them most in their growth. Usually, I start by putting participants with others who are similar in some way, to provide some level of comfort and easy connection. This is a period of opening and developing self-awareness. By the second and third rotation, I am looking for pairings that might be more complex—different personalities, different ways of approaching work. I am always taking their goals and the organizational goals into consideration while looking for opportunities to jostle the individual from a stagnant worldview.

An optimal peer coaching relationship:

- requires good contracting between the individuals, which should specify what the insight partner is looking for help with and what type of feedback is desired. Then, when the peer coach provides feedback, the partners are responding to a specific request. One should not give feedback that hasn't been asked for.

- builds opportunities for real dialogue and mutual insight. The relationship gets built on trust and confidentiality through a nonthreatening approach.

- encourages reflection. We need to learn to pause and reflect in order to make the necessary learning connections.

- is a developmental strategy where individuals benefit from learning together through a shared experience. In situations where individuals get to see each other in the course of their work, i.e., are in a project meeting together, the peer coach can provide useful feedback and examples if the partner is open to it.

- fosters collaboration. Healthy collaboration can be difficult in organizational life. This is an opportunity to learn what it might look like at its best.

- is not part of the evaluation process in performance management. Individuals providing the coaching should not be asked to provide feedback for their *Insight Partners'* performance review. If they are asked to do this, they must consider the confidentialities and the special relationship they share before drawing up their remarks.

Some participants take this time very seriously, using it to benefit them for years to come. Others merely check the box on another responsibility. But in the end, most say that it was one of the most important parts of the process. These are relationships that are developed much further than most they experience in their organizational life.

Journaling

Journal writing has been around for many centuries. A quick internet search will show that journals date back to the likes of the Han dynasty, Marcus Aurelius, and the wife of Fujiwara, a Japanese statesman. Famous journalers include Marie Curie, Charles Darwin, Leonardo Da Vinci, Thomas Edison, Albert Einstein, Anne Frank, George Lucas, and Anais Nin. The University of Rochester Medical Center supports journaling on its website, defining it as "simply writing down your thoughts and feelings to understand them more clearly" (Ballas 2018).

In the 1960s, Ira Progoff, a New York City psychologist, focused on the therapeutic benefits of reflective writing and made his *Intensive Journal* method popular through workshops and classes (Adams 2018). Serendipitously, Progoff was a student of Carl Jung's. He wanted journalers to become more structured, to go deeper in writing about the life they wanted and the challenges they were having in reaching their desires. Today, it is hard to get people in organizations to want to use a journal. In this modern age, we seem to run on autopilot a good portion of the day, not fully aware of what we're doing or why we're doing it. Taking time to reflect is almost a ridiculous suggestion. But reflecting, quieting the mind, is the very behavior that

> "I should advise you to put it all down as beautifully as you can, in some beautifully bound book."
>
> C. G. JUNG

enables us to see potential problems, mistakes, possibilities, connections, and feelings of great importance. It's the opportunity to listen to the small inner voice. And, if we don't stop to take stock and be responsible for the life we're living, we'll wake up one day to find we're living someone else's. When we're journaling with serious intention, we go back over what we've written to find patterns and comments that stand out or even surprise us. These continuous reflections over time lead us to new revelations and understanding of ourselves and the deeper meaning of our lives. They help us to see the pathway to our individuation.

An article in the American Psychological Association journal titled "Writing to Heal" shares research that shows the multiple physical, emotional, and social healing benefits of journaling. Jung, Progoff, and so many other authors, psychologists, and educators have field tested the value of the practice. I find reflective writing to be one of the most important aspects of transformational work, and Insight Group Coaching encourages this as a regular part of the yearlong process.

The participants are given a journal and encouraged to start writing in it a little each week. It is suggested that they note things that surprise them, anger them, worry them, or resonate with them.

> "Until you make the unconscious conscious, it will direct your life and you will call it fate."
>
> C. G. JUNG

Because we discuss personality and values in our first meeting, I often suggest participants start writing about insights relative to this data. They might use questions like the following as prompts: *What made immediate sense in your feedback and why? What behaviors or motivations didn't resonate with you?* I follow those questions with, *Try to imagine a scenario when it actually did or could play itself out?* Based on what comes out in the writing, they are to follow up on feelings, questions, and concerns with more writing. Seeing their values show up in support of what they pay attention to, what they care about, and what is personally satisfying, or not, is very informative. And the next layer of writing (and for some, talking it out) can elucidate one or two very important pieces of information, bringing about very useful insight and consideration for next steps.

In one situation when I reviewed the values (VAL®) assessment data with a 40-year-old man, he couldn't make sense of his core operational values. It turned out that he was a very clear "Intuitive" Type® and hadn't paid much attention to how he incorporated his beliefs day-to-day. His focus was on the long view. He agreed to take on the assignment of journaling any experience of his top three values in the following week.

He emailed me in two days to say that he was astonished to realize these values were clearly his motivational base, having discovered many ways in which he employed them. He decided to take the challenge further and look at the next set of three values. He became a believer in the effects of journaling very quickly but, more importantly, he began shifting some of his priorities, which reduced his stress level. It wasn't that he was any less busy, but he felt a real connection to the work he was doing. He was reenergized around his goals.

I suggest that all of the participants do some of this type of testing to ensure their prioritization reflects what is real in their lives. Sometimes people get stuck in reflecting some ideal instead. To gain the most value from our work together I continuously encourage participants to make this reflective writing a regular part of their weekly activities.

I share with them the following suggestions for gaining comfort in journaling:

- Pay attention to anything that annoys you this week and write it down. Describe it as fully as you can.

- Note what feelings surfaced in your experiences with others. Were you surprised by them? Do your core values explain these feelings?

- Consider your best decisions and worst decisions of the last month or year and write about those. What made them good or bad? Are those reasons expressed through your core values[1]? In other words, if you made the decision to take on extra responsibilities at work last month, when you look at your core values, do they support that as a good decision, or do you see things like *family* and *freedom* staring back at you like blinking red lights, resonating why this might not have been a good idea for you?

By reviewing their core values against these notes, the participants start to see patterns that either reinforce these core values or bring to light a value or two that is very important but has been unconscious. Ideas for

---

1   An exercise I learned from my work at ORA, Consultants. They were the developers of the VAL®, which is now managed and sold under Golden Assessments.

eliciting insights develop from the experience with the group each month, where they hear about other's test cases and epiphanies.

Depending on the group, some other prompts I might suggest include:

- Where/how was I particularly strong this week/month?
- How does that connect to who I am? (e.g., Type®, Values, Roles that I play?)
- Where/how do I wish I would have been stronger (had more impact) this month? How does that relate to my Type®/Values?
- What most concerns me about my work and my future?
- What will I do with this information?
- What are my key strengths?
- Who demonstrated a skill that I wish I had? What action do I want to take as a result?
- What leaders do I most admire in this organization? Why? Other leaders? Historical leaders? Why?
- What is a driving, unrelenting question in my mind?

Journaling is definitely key to bringing about insights, but some participants note that it is hard to commit to the time and it is hard to figure out what to write when they do finally sit down with their journal. I advise that it's best to start by quieting your mind and releasing yourself from all the *shoulds* and *musts* that arise. Setting aside the expectation for perfection is important. I support that by reassuring that full sentences, punctuation, and even capital letters don't matter. Just write. Write about the discomfort you feel in writing or reflecting. It is uncomfortable because it is a new way of paying attention to one's psyche and the ego-Self[2] axis.

> "The only questions that really matter are the ones you ask yourself."
>
> Ursula K. Le Guin

---

2   Creating more conversation between the ego and the Self is what enables us to bring deep ideas and archetypal understanding to consciousness.

In each group, there is usually at least one individual who really takes to the writing and finds it especially revealing and invaluable. And, there is typically one who doesn't get into it at all, and the journal is left empty throughout the year in spite of my prompts. But all is not lost. They are still getting provoked and challenged. Without this provocation, we all stay small, lacking agility, and stuck in our certainty.

In one group of senior women, there was an individual who was not happy with how things were going in the organization for her.

> "Without the reflecting consciousness of man the world is a gigantic meaningless machine, for as far as we know man is the only creature that can discover 'meaning.'"
>
> C. G. JUNG, LETTER TO
> ERICH NEUMANN, MARCH 1959

In our first one-on-one meeting, she complained that she didn't even know why she was chosen for the group. Of course, it had been clearly stated that all of the participants were considered high potentials and were written into succession plans. She had been personally invited by a high-ranking female physician leader to take part in the process. But she was not convinced. The other nine women interacted with high energy, and she sat back with a pout on her face. From time to time, she would make a terse comment. I thought she was miserable. She came across as knowing it all and not very interested. I decided to let the energy of the group work on her for a while rather than step right in. In our one-on-ones, I would challenge her—a bit cautiously at first as I didn't want to scare her off, but later more directly. I told her she appeared very unhappy and I felt it was impacting others. I asked her what she thought was creating her discontent. She replied that she thought it might be time to go back to therapy. It felt like more of a question than an answer. I thought it might just be a crutch, but I said, "Maybe." I suggested she do some journaling, as I expected that would be enjoyable to her Type®. Yet her general malaise had her quite out of sorts and confused. She was stuck. Others thought her aloof. Then, when we did our group check-in three months later, I finally saw her smile. She engaged with the group and seemed more relaxed. When we talked about her shift in attitude, she said she finally realized she was blaming the group for her own frustrations. She couldn't see it because she wasn't ready to see it. She wanted to believe everyone was as miserable as she was—they just weren't willing to admit it. A couple others in the group that had the courage and had gained enough insight over the months had challenged her in a very considerate way to try to look at things differently. In the three months between the ninth and 12th month (10th meeting), she took on the journaling in a deep and meaningful way. She asked herself some hard questions and took a day off to answer them in silence and in a space without distraction. She didn't like some of the answers she came up with but came to see it was up to her alone to make some changes in her behavior and attitude.

Famed Jungian analyst, Marion Woodman, encourages us to think about the journal as a mirror and allow it to work its magic on us. She says,

> Facing our dark sides is painful. It is easier to know so much and no more. It is easier to turn away from our own swamp of anguish and aggression and say, "It doesn't matter. I've got friends. I'm adjusted to my job. Everyone likes me." The mirror will not let us off the hook. It says, "It does matter. If you're not experiencing life, it does matter. Where was your own laughter today? Where are your tears? Why did you betray yourself? Haven't you got the guts to face your own truth?" (Woodman, 1982)

Leaders who can do this work of looking at themselves and knowing themselves are great models, helping us all to bring the stories of our lives to some useful expression. This is how we do the work of self-awareness and self-management. It is not that we must change who we are but that we become conscious of who we are. It is healing work. It is how we come into our own authority.

"Our wisdom is all mixed up with what we call our neurosis. Our brilliance, our juiciness, our spiciness, is all mixed up with our craziness and our confusion, and therefore it doesn't do any good to try to get rid of our so-called negative aspects, because in that process we also get rid of our basic wonderfulness. We can lead our life so as to become more awake to who we are and what we're doing rather than trying to improve or change or get rid of who we are or what we're doing. The key is to wake up, to become more alert, more inquisitive and curious about ourselves."

PEMA CHODRON

Books and Articles

I generally choose all of the books and articles we will use in a group, as I am working off what has been effective in the past and knowledge of this organization (goals, vision, mission, leadership competencies, etc.) from the contracting conversations with HR and the business sponsor. My familiarity of an expansive number of resources enables me to organize a resonant and meaningful plan. But every so often someone makes a suggestion, and if it seems a good fit with our goals and the work in front of us, I will include it. In one such instance, I began using *Multipliers* by Liz Wiseman, and it has become quite a regular. One group participant was so taken with the ideas of how we can either multiply or diminish others that he used it with several teams and wrote a blog about it.

Another book that I have used since the first contracted group is *Leadership and Self-Deception* by the Arbinger Group. Through the fabled story, individuals learn about how we justify ourselves, thereby damaging relationships, and how we collude with others in the demise of collaboration. We discuss the "better than," "smarter than," "more experienced than," ways in which we see ourselves at times and how that isolates us from others. While these personas (masks, splinter personalities emerging from a complex) support our ego, they do little for the relationships we need in the collaborative work model of today. Once seen, it is hard to go fully unconscious about our behaviors in the future. If we can actually take a hard look at our projections and see how they're hurting us, we can adjust and reap immediate benefits personally and in our teams. It's important to realize that projections are how we establish relationships, so it is not that we want to eradicate them, but we do need to withdraw them at some point in order to let a relationship of integrity form.

> "The best political, social, and spiritual work we can do is to withdraw the projections of our own shadow onto others."
> C.G. JUNG

Two participants who were particularly impacted by the reading and their experience also decided to get copies of the book for their teams. They got a lot of mileage out of sharing their own insights and discussing the concepts with team members. The reinforcement of concepts was valuable for all, creating more open discussion and a supportive environment.

Having a core set of books and articles will further establish your approach and purpose. By core, I am referring to those materials that you use from group to group because they are so salient to the success of leadership and your philosophical premise. They should clearly support one another and fit with your framework. As the group progresses through the assigned readings, participants will see the threads of values, leadership ethics, and behaviors you're advocating, and they should align with the organization's core values and leadership competencies. I often offer up podcasts, TED talks, and movies as a good e-learning option and reinforcement or alternative to all the reading.

Core Models

In addition to the books and other resources, you bring various models into play and encourage participants to test them out in their day-to-day work. I like to start simply and provide some core models that an individual can access easily and regularly in order to build sound management and leadership capability. I will share three of my favorites.

You will likely be familiar with the Johari window and its four quadrants of *Open, Blind, Secret* and *Closed*. It is a favorite of mine as it aligns nicely with my Jungian foundation and the analytical communication model, noted in the first two books of the series. I also find it intersects well with the emotional intelligence conversation that is woven throughout the process and the core book, *Leadership and Self-Deception*, mentioned above.

The groups that have less management experience benefit from the *GROW* model. It is a great basic focusing on *Goals, Realities, Options* and *Will* that can help you get through most difficult conversations without having to memorize scripted paragraphs or use fancy charts to accomplish your task. It also aligns with my theoretical underpinnings and encouragement of mutual respect and clean communications (aka, managing our projections). The model has a set of questions that aligns with each of the four focal areas, but there is room for experimentation with one's own language, curiosities, and needs.

The final model I want to share is known as the "3 Cs." It is a relationship building model that I designed for cross-cultural communication, but over time it has expanded to encompass most relationship work. In this model we look at the build of *Curiosity, Cultivation* and *Collaboration* (table 2) and the *competencies, knowledge, values,* and *qualities* (table 3) that evolve these behaviors. Individuals who want to be seen as open, as "learners" with the ability to develop teams and networks, for example, align with the three "C's". They use the "knower" column[3] (table 2) as red flags to help them see where they are falling into negative behaviors or a *victim* mentality. We often tie this in with our stakeholder management work.

While this model is more complex, it is one that really helps people to evolve and develop their emotional intelligence, if they're up for experimenting with it. As with the others, it builds nicely on the core book messages and Analytical Framework.

Table 2

Relationship Management I

"Learner" [Player]	"Knower" [Victim]
Skills:	*Red flags:*
Curiosity	o Disinterest o Irrelevance o Superiority
Cultivation	o Minimization o Trivialization o Denigration
Collaboration	o Distancing o Separation o Isolation

*Designed by Janet Steinwedel, PhD, for Leader's Insight, LLC

---

3   The nine knower traits come from the work of Milton Bennett and his framework on Intercultural Sensitivity, and stimulated much of my thinking in developing this model.

Table 3

Relationship Management II

How to be a "learner" [player]

Ethno-relative Behaviors	Competencies	Knowledge	Underlying Values	Qualities
Curiosity	•Inquiry skills •Listening skills •Self-awareness •Self-development •Discernment	•One's own culture •Other cultures	•Learning •Knowledge	•Humility •Courage
Cultivation	•Understanding others (needs, customs, values) •Patience •Optimism	•The other (internally & externally) •How to request & invite rather than tell or sell	•Love •Pleasure •Self-worth	•Appreciation •Gratitude
Collaboration	•Relationship building •Agility (flexibility, adaptability, facilitation) •Motivating others •Personal disclosure	•Personal strengths •The other's skills, knowledge, capability, etc. •Integration as opposed to conversion	•Achievement •Learning •Developing relationships •Others' ideas/perspectives	•Respect •Generosity

*Designed by Janet Steinwedel, PhD, for Leader's Insight, LLC

Closing

While I've given you a little of what happens at the end, let me tell you about the typical 10th meeting in the 12th month. At this time, group members have spent nine consecutive months meeting together and three months continuing their peer coaching and integration of tools and techniques. Usually they have had a one-on-one with me prior to the ninth meeting or just following as a means to tying up their experience. Some contracts have me meeting more often with each participant, and then I might have sessions throughout this three-month period. In some groups, there will be a final reading that we discuss as part of their last check-in. But for the most part, the last meeting is part celebration and part planning for how to continue to gain value from this network.

In terms of the celebration, the managers of the participants join us for 30 minutes either in person or via videoconference. This is the one time I also allow for teleconference calls in order to accommodate all possible guests. My HR contact, the CHRO, and the sponsor are also invited. I facilitate a question-and-answer period, giving the managers the opportunity to learn more about their employees' experience. Since the participants did a short presentation in the ninth month, they are quite prepared for the questions. I also encourage them to revisit favorite articles and books that they might like to talk about. Sometimes I get asked a question. When appropriate, I give first dibs at an answer to the group, but then provide minimal additional thoughts. The important thing is that this is not about the facilitator. It is an opportunity for the members to shine and be seen as mature contributors on the topic of leadership (and the key competencies that were our focus). This is generally fun for all and a nice ritual for completion. In a few cases, organizations have chosen to have a manager check-in earlier in the process, but never before the sixth meeting. In support of my philosophical position, the conversation and energy would end up being too egocentric (i.e.: Are they getting "it," is my participating manager smart enough, did I choose the right person?) But by the end, the integration of ego and Self is more developed, and members present themselves more from their own authority than from a position of compliance (e.g.: I'm a good student, I did all the work, I have the right answer—or the answer you want to hear, etc.) as is, unfortunately, too common in organizational life.

Finally, we delve into ideas for continuation. A majority of participants inevitably want to determine how they will stay connected. They have experienced the value of the peer coaching and the expansion of their network, and they realize it would be a mistake to let it go too soon. For some, this is their first attempt at developing a useful network of mutuality. The group brainstorms ways of staying connected and makes some commitments to one another. Typically, someone takes the responsibility for setting up a next meeting. Now they are on to the next iteration of their relationships and expanding what they have learned.

Operationalizing a process like this takes a lot of time and skill. It is not something you just decide to do because it sounds like fun. Sorting out the important objectives and organizational expectations, including using their language and competencies is an important first step. Following up with the mix of materials that will best serve the goals and managing the participants' responsibilities to provide opportunities for leadership, collaboration, and followership within the group are all very key to the end value. Threading the insights from the participants' assessments and building on those tools throughout the effort strengthens their self-awareness and self-knowledge and builds their confidence for the activities of the last two meetings and beyond. And ensuring that journaling is experienced as a learning tool to be used during this process and onward can bind all the efforts together for optimal and continued results. Of course, the peer-to-peer and one-on-one coaching is critical for continuity of engagement and pulling through the threads and curiosities of each participant at an individual needs level.

As I've cautioned before, the coach/facilitator needs to do a lot of self-work first. Too much ego and not enough experience will make it merely a set of activities at best, and at worse a complete charade.

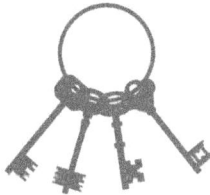

Questions to consider

What tools, books, activities might make up core aspects of a group of your design?

What are the most important threads you would want to pull through such a process?

III

Understanding and Managing the Dynamics of Groups

"In my innocence I thought that I myself had broken the ice and that no more obstacles would be placed in my path. I was quite sure that they were all willing to tell me what I wished to know."

ELENORE SMITH BOWEN, *RETURN TO LAUGHTER*

As the facilitator of a group, you will face a lot of unknowns. No matter how much preparation you undertake prior to the first meeting, there is no way of predicting exactly what will happen when the group comes together. Some groups are more naturally optimistic, enthusiastic, and forward looking; some are more cautious, reserved, and anxious. The possibilities are, of course, endless. But, in order to prepare for a new group, we start by working with what we know. For example, you will know something about the diversity of the group, and this is important information. From a wide lens my groups are generally mixed gender or all women, and they're multidisciplinary, cross-cultural, and often from multiple locations. Getting more granular, we can start by looking at the Personality Types® within a group.

Diversity and Typology®

We spoke earlier of assessments. I have used a variety of instruments with groups, including the ESCI®, Hogan®, DISC® and Strengthsfinder®.

You will have your preferences. Most often I am using the MBTI®[1] and VAL®. They are a nice complement to one another with the values often supporting a person's Type® or expressing why the person might "appear" quite different within a Type®. The MBTI® is a long-standing, widely used tool because it is so robust. It has made it much easier for organizations and teams to leverage their talent, discuss diversity, and manage conflict. The many great support materials available enable more personal insights with increased efficiency. There are three I particularly like to use: *In the Grip: Understanding Type, Stress, and the Inferior Function* by Naomi Quenk; *Introduction to Type and Emotional Intelligence* by Roger Pearman; and *Introduction to Type and Innovation* by Damian Killen and Gareth Williams. After a clear introduction of Type® to each participant, we continue to work with the information throughout the process.

In most groups there are several people that have taken the MBTI® before. In most cases I find they have not delved in too far. They seem to enjoy coming back to it and having the opportunity to further work with and understand its value.

So, I have information from the HR and sponsor conversations, I have the Type® and VAL® information, and I have insights from my first meetings with each participant. This gives me some data to work with as I try to piece together the group profile and anticipate its dynamics. I often check first to see how many "Extraverts" and "Introverts" I have. Knowing that will tell me something about the energy I can expect.

> "Another way of looking at our life is to confess that we swim continuously in force fields of energy."
>
> JAMES HOLLIS

---

1   There has been some confusion about the MBTI® with the 5 factor Personality Inventories ("Big Five"). It is important not to confuse the two approaches to looking at Personality. The MBTI® is a predictive and dynamic approach to looking at preferences. It is a tool for self-awareness and does not correlate with effectiveness. The 5 factor tools, based on a different theory, are evaluative, and they measure traits: openness, conscientiousness, extraversion, agreeableness, and neuroticism. These measurements are used to determine one's effectiveness. It is unethical to make hiring and promotion decisions based on one's MBTI® results.

An Attitude of Action or Reflection

I agree with Daryl Sharp's observation that "No one, of course, is only 'Introverted' or 'Extraverted.' Although each of us, in the process of following our dominant inclination or adapting to our immediate world, invariably develops one attitude more than the other, the opposite attitude is still potentially there" (Sharp 1987). That said, it is useful to consider the numbers in the group of those living a dominant "Extraverted" or "Introverted" preference. More "Extraverts" will mean an objective, external focus, whereas a majority "Introverted" group will mean a subjective, internal focus. I have never had an all "Extraverted" or all "Introverted" group. And, I have only had one group that leaned more heavily in the "Introverted" direction. This required something different from me (an "Extravert") in my facilitation style and in my reflection work after our group meetings. While we are all one-sided in how we see things, this additional weighted differentiation made it all the more important that I take time to consider what I wasn't automatically seeing. My tendency was to not keenly consider the "Introvert's" needs. It wasn't that I *couldn't* do that; it was that I hadn't been motivated to do it. I also learned that I was more tired than usual after the group session. The pace was slower. It took more out of me. That in itself is an important insight, as it is typical for "Introverts" to have that experience from group interaction all the time.

In organizations it is often thought that "Extraverted" personalities are better. Indeed, in groups "Extraverts" tend to be the ones to liven things up. But one is not better than the other, and we learn a lot from being able to flex our own preferred style. With my "Introverted" group I learned to be more patient after posing a question, enabling participants to more carefully consider their response, which is their nature. I was more deliberate in giving them their responsibilities for facilitating pieces of the discussion, so they were ready to jump in on cue. We took more pauses and sometimes wrote thoughts down before having to express them. As a group, we had some very rich conversations about the challenges for "Introverts" in organizations and how they could not only survive but thrive in organizational life.

My journaling after meetings provided an important mirror for my subjective view of things. It ensured that I didn't get triggered or come up with the same "Extraverted" solutions but instead, regularly considered an opposite approach. "What we are not conscious of in ourselves is by definition beyond our control. When the undeveloped attitude is constellated, we are prey to all kinds of disruptive emotions—we are 'complexed'" (Sharp 1987). This reflective experience enhanced how I prepare for and lead all subsequent groups.

Other Aspects of Type® To Consider

Type® data will also tell me about how this group tends to take in information—do members prefer "Sensing" (concrete and experiential) over "Intuition" (big picture and interrelationships-oriented) or vice versa? I will have some idea of their preference for decision-making and if that is more logical and objective from the "Thinking" orientation or more harmony seeking and values laden, a function of subjective judgment, from the "Feeling" polarity. I've only had one group that had more participants with a preference for "Feeling" than "Thinking." And here I want to offer a reminder that we can't confuse emotions with feeling. Emotions are affect, which comes from triggering a complex. A complex is a structure that forms in the unconscious of the psyche from early experiences. It holds a lot of energy that we don't know what to do with and forms the basis for our reactions. For example, if a person is afraid of the disapproval of others (perhaps because that person grew up with pressure to be a perfect child) and acts on that fear, he or she is suffering from a complex. All Types® get triggered and all experience emotions. "Feeling" Types® are not *more* emotional, and they can even be cold in certain situations, but how they feel about things (what they value or those close to them value) drives their decisions. Hollis has noted that we don't create our feelings, but that our feelings are a qualitative analysis by the psyche.

In my clearly "Extraverted Feeling" group, the members' check-in was always high energy. They shared their personal perspectives of how the leaders were undervaluing them or not demonstrating caring of others. I always felt it right to give them time to let everything out and then to ask why they thought these issues held so much importance to them. Working with their VAL® reports was an important part of our work. Assisting them in connecting back to their passions and understanding their projections provided good growth for the whole group. In this "Feeling" group, I also observed how it took more effort to get into the data and the group often shared how members felt about the reading assignments before getting more logically discriminating. Working with their VAL® reports strengthened their authenticity and confidence.

Finally, by taking a high-level look at Type®, I will know in general how participants are oriented toward life, that is if they are more "Judging" ("J")—organized, planful, and scheduled—or if they are more "Perceiving" ("P")[2]—open-ended, spontaneous, and emergent. Groups more populated with "Judging" Types® like our meetings to be well-designed and are natural timekeepers. Most of my groups have been more heavily weighted in the direction of "J." With the groups that have three or more "P's," the dynamics change. Managing emergence and spontaneity into our time together becomes both a challenge and an opportunity. Often in corporate group work, things naturally move along in an orderly fashion, and we develop a routine, but when the number of "P's" rise, we have to bring some shift to how the meeting runs. They enjoy it when I start a meeting saying, "Today let's do something different." Then I've got their attention.

> "There is no change from darkness to light, or from inertia to movement without emotion."
>
> C.G. JUNG

This diversity of Type® provides many valuable lessons, allowing participants to experience "otherness" on friendly terms. Even groups that look quite a lot alike, at least on paper, or culturally, exhibit clear differentiation. Values, interests, experiences, and needs of the participants will all impact the dynamics.

Managing the Dynamics of a Difficult Situation

Not all groups run smoothly. Being prepared to manage awkward situations can be a necessary skill. Here's an example: A young man in one of my groups (an overall younger group than I usually have) sent me an email seeking clarification of what he was responsible for doing for our

---

2   The "Judging/Perceiving" scale was not Jung's, but an addition of the Myers-Briggs team. Jung's work pointed to Sensing and Intuition as functions of Perception and Thinking and Feeling as functions of Judgment.

next group meeting. He cc'd the rest of the group, noting that if he was confused, others probably were too. I send notes to group members after every session with an outline of what is expected for the next meeting. I have found this to be a clear, succinct way to convey the same information to all participants, allowing them to refer to it as needed. Also, this approach has helped avoid the rush to conclude when nearing the two-hour mark and participants may tend toward preoccupation with asking how to prepare for the next meeting. This young man received the notes with my expectations but sought clarity. I provided this to him by sending further notes with some additional direction. In the next group meeting he spoke up, quickly noting that he'd talked with others who were also unsure of my expectations and also happened to feel I was expecting too much work. I asked what was unclear. I am typically aware that as an "Intuitive" (albeit a *concrete,* Intuitive on the MBTI® Step II) I sometimes don't make clear enough links for some. I reminded them that this was not a classroom and I would not treat them as my students. One person chimed in, agreeing that their workloads were too heavy. The situation provided a great teaching moment. But what did I want to teach? (Teaching is part of the *Coaching* aspect of the CAF model, known as *Education* in the Jungian model.) And what was the truth of what he was saying?

Here are some of the thoughts (projections and reflections) that drove my feedback to the participant:

- He is overwhelmed with work and clearly wants me to tell him what to do.

- He wants to let me know that I am not doing a very good job of being clear (a projection that takes the responsibility off of him and puts it on me). I am also thinking that it is more personal in that I'm not providing the clarity that *he* is comfortable with.

- If I give him what he wants, he won't stretch out of his "STJ" ("Sensing," "Thinking," "Judging") preferences—concrete, linear and the way things should be, and he'll likely always want something more from me.

- The group is a strong "STJ" group, and he could easily bring others into collusion with him.

- It seems that this person in particular needs to work on his "Intuition," "Feeling," and "Perception." He needs to learn when to set knowing, and the scientific approach aside.

- Anyone can follow precise directions, but that wouldn't bring the most robust conversations to bear or help him to grow out of a childhood model.

First, I checked my own emotional state. How was I experiencing this participant and his message? When I considered my state to be rather neutral, I continued. My feedback to the group was direct, yet reassuring, noting that I would always tell the participants what my expectations were and that they needed to commit to carefully reviewing the follow-up note I sent after sessions. I encouraged them to talk with their peer coach and other group members in an effort to clarify what they didn't understand (not to commiserate). I emphasized that I would treat them like adults and trust if they didn't get to something, it was because it wasn't possible to do so. And I said that while I did need to know if it really was too much work or I wasn't being clear, I expected that they would make every effort to take responsibility for their part. I took the opportunity to also remind them that while I wanted to know what *they* wanted to talk about—what was interesting and compelling to them—this talk of what exactly am I supposed to do only took time away from having value-added conversation. Finally, I suggested that they take what didn't make sense immediately, that which was paradoxical even, and write about it, talk about it, mull it over, because I was sure they would come up with a fine response and take a good next step. And then I asked them to take back the projection, that is, understand this matter was probably not about what I was doing *to* them. This is the work. It was up to me to help them to realize that making others responsible for them kept them in an inferior position and wouldn't enable them to grow their leadership. I finished by asking for questions and to honestly tell me if something I said didn't make sense. These are golden opportunities, because when one sees bad habits or defensive responses when they are occurring, group members are more likely to be able to let them go. It is that being present to the discomfort and having access to a better way that enables transformations.

Later, in talking with the young man, I asked him about his level of work activity right now and inquired if it was a good time for him to be part of the group. I asked for his feedback about what I said to the group. I felt we had a very good conversation and a much better understanding of how the group would work and why. Several months had passed when he revealed to me that he was making excuses for himself and explained that he became more aware of how he does that when he feels unprepared or overwhelmed. That was a very useful revelation for him. It was also a relief to me that the whole group wasn't usurped by one member. I kept the necessary level of control without being controlling. And, I felt that the experience provided a great opportunity for us all to work on getting unstuck together.

Maturity

This brings me to another dynamic that the facilitator must face, which involves the maturity levels within the group. This can be affected by age, experience, length of time in leadership roles, opportunities to get feedback over their careers, etc. Because the individuals are considered high potential and range from director level to senior vice presidents, they generally hit some threshold of maturity that is necessary for effective behavior. In other words, they're not notably defensive, they are respectful of others, they generally listen well enough. When there is a noticeable lack of maturity, individuals make excuses for themselves, they blame the system or others for their inability to perform well, get heard, or get promoted. The maturity level typically shows up from person to person, not by groups, as in the previous example where one individual's lack of sufficient maturity showed up in his struggle to be flexible and responsible under pressure. When it is by group, it shows up relatively early in the group process. Sometimes I see it in biases and general pessimism.

In one group, I experienced a fair amount of resistance. Unlike the example above, there were several individuals involved, and they were primarily complaining about leadership. There had been some significant changes in senior leadership in recent years, and it seemed that they could do no right by these particular participants. In their view, nobody in the organization was happy. I believed that this was their projections and their way of voicing discomfort with change. Yet, I prefer to reflect first, especially as in this case, when I sensed that I was annoyed with what felt like an immature attitude. Since I knew and respected most of the leadership, I wondered if I was just feeling defensive. Was I not taking into consideration what it was like to work in this organization? One group work expert sheds light on how to handle this scenario:

> "One of the most powerful ways to intervene when you are experiencing strong feelings over what you perceive to be resistance is to deal with your own feelings and possible defensive reactions to the situation. If you ignore your reactions, you are leaving yourself out of the interactions that occur in the group. Furthermore, by giving the members your reactions, you are modeling a direct style of dealing with conflict and resistance, rather than bypassing it" (Schneider-Corey and Corey, 1997).

As the Corey's suggest, I decided to let the group know how I was feeling. I told the participants that I'd had a lot of good experiences with many of the leaders, and while I don't work inside the organization day in and day out, I felt pretty positive about the direction things were going. I told them I wanted to hear more about why they might feel differently and that it was safe to voice their opinions. I reminded them that they, too, are leaders and that others might find some of their behaviors frustrating. I suggested that they consider how they would want other leaders, hearing such concerns, to respond. Before we ended, I referred them to our reading of the Arbinger book, *Leadership and Self-Deception*, and suggested they discuss their thoughts in their peer-to-peer sessions as they relate to that model. In the wrap-up, I noted that we would start our check-in at the next session with any insights that came up. One thing I was aware of was that I wanted to support the group in being able to be vulnerable, not scare them into defending themselves. Giving them some time and a model to work with diffused their reactions and helped them with their personal and collective growth.

Depending on age and experience, many of our participants come in the doors early in the process ready with answers. But teaching them to take a moment to devise a thoughtful question is much more interesting for everyone. And, when you have a participant who falls into playing some kind of archetypal role, such as the sooth—the wise one— redirecting that person can help you manage the dynamics and the experience for everyone. The participation and engagement of all participants is very important. Everyone needs to take part and experiment with new approaches to engaging the others. The reading, questioning, and presenting get them prepared for a good group experience. It furthers their commitment, develops their presence and their self-awareness.

Valuing Vulnerability Supports Good Group Dynamics

I have found it useful as the facilitator to both model vulnerability and to help group members see the value in it for their leadership. Two of today's high-profile speakers with unique voices in the field of leadership and self-development are David Whyte and Brené Brown. They both extol the necessity of vulnerability and the importance of taking some emotional risks, allowing for some personal exposure, and finding *wholeheartedness*. When we are busy, on overload, checking boxes, we easily find ourselves to be pessimistic and lacking energy. Whyte shares from personal experience that "the antidote to exhaustion is not rest, but wholeheartedness."[3] It would be impossible to love what we are doing all day, every day, but when we find little passion for our work over long periods of time, we are setting ourselves up for failure of one kind or another.

> "There are many tenets of Wholeheartedness, but at its very core is vulnerability and worthiness; facing uncertainty, exposure, and emotional risks, and knowing that I am enough." (Brown 2012)

Few people actually do feel as if they are enough. And those who act as if they do, often err on the side of being too much—possibly even arrogant and grandstanding. Many try to create a life without exposing their softer side, without vulnerability. "Don't let them see you sweat." "Man up." "Don't let your guard down." And yet, we know a life without vulnerability, without being true to ourselves, is not a real life at all.

---

3   You will see several quotes from talks given by David Whyte. He has a beautiful way of expressing the human condition both in person and in his books. I have given "The Three Marriages," to some of my groups. I encourage you to pick up a book, or audio talk, ie: "Clear Mind, Wild Heart," and if possible, go on one of his walking tours.

Organizational life can have one walking around in a bit of a trance. I'm reminded of the Dunkin' Donuts commercial, with the half-asleep employee mumbling, *Got to make the donuts.* Single-mindedness, while it has its value, generally keeps us small and disheartened. Being in a trance is another way of armoring up so that no one can penetrate us. I have heard participants warn their colleagues to *stay under the radar* or *just get the job done.* But that is not the life most of us had imagined when we took our first professional job and it is not what most want as we climb the career ladder. It is just this kind of banality that keeps leaders from bringing out the best in their teams and their companies.

> "Vulnerability is not a weakness, a passing indisposition, or something we can arrange to do without, vulnerability is the underlying, ever present and abiding undercurrent of our natural state."
>
> DAVID WHYTE

Over time, many learn that while organizations say they want employees to speak up and to tell the truth, to have courage, when they do, it often results in uncomfortable outcomes—dis-ease. Much of my work with teams is due to such *diseases,* and it is usually brought up in group discussions. It is our job as facilitators and coaches to hold up the metaphorical mirror and help individuals see the role that they play in the dis-ease of their organization—to help them see the value in pushing through uncertainty, taking some emotional risks and using their vulnerability to see practical solutions to the challenges they face. These are the efforts that lead to wholehearted leadership.

One participant said to me at the end of a yearlong process, "Sometimes I walked away [from our sessions] thinking I was TOO transparent, but I eventually got over it." Her transparency and wholeheartedness, in fact, often helped others to have more real conversations, by modeling the courage they needed to speak up. When we encourage vulnerability and individuals take risks to be more vulnerable, we arrive at a more meaningful and wholehearted place. These are the necessary conditions for transformational growth.

David Whyte describes what he calls the *Courageous Conversation*—of which the first point is to "stop having the conversation you've been having because you're likely stuck." Developing constructive conversational technique is something we can work on all our lives.

Like many of my clients, you may have read or heard of Fierce Conversations (Susan Scott), Authentic Conversations (James Showkeir), Crucial Conversations (Kerry Patterson, Joseph Grenny, Ron McMillan, Al Switzler), or Difficult Conversations (Douglas Stone, Bruce Patton), all of these processes and persuasions are designed to help us enter more meaningful and more courageous conversations. I am particularly fond of the courageous approach as it tells us right up front that *this* conversation requires heart.

> "To love at all is to be vulnerable."
> C. S. Lewis

Wholeheartedness. Whyte directs us to *hazard* ourselves—to take risks and be more vulnerable in the conversation. When we do that—hazard ourselves, risk—we become more vulnerable and honest in all of our conversations. We own our feelings, thoughts and desires. When we make courageous conversations more the norm we help reduce the dis-ease in organizations.

Authenticity and Courageous Conversation

The loose-tight approach that I take with my groups puts us all on our edges and pushes us to speak what is top of mind, what feels important in that moment and germane to the conversation at hand. The facilitator should not have prepared speeches. Preparation should consist of rereading books and articles, reviewing participant assessment reports and interview conversations, and keeping past group discussions in mind. As the facilitator, I take a risk right along with the participants by sharing what is being summoned by the underlying invitation of the group in that moment. If we're all truly listening and authentically responding, our vulnerability is keenly available in service to us. Both facilitator and participant might feel worried that they'll say something that they will regret. Being authentic does not mean we say just any thought that comes up. Being authentic comes from knowing who we are and from doing the difficult work of understanding our biases, triggers, and needs. Then when we speak from that sense of clarity, we do not speak to degrade or hurt others, we speak to let others see us. Often this risking of ourselves enables a mutual vulnerability. I'm reminded of an early conversation in this book about *kinship libido*—the essence of which gives off a creative energy in service to our highest aspirations and our best selves.

Whyte tells a story of the time he spent with a wise mentor, Br.David Steindl-Rast, and they spoke of Whyte's exhaustion. One of the things Steindl-Rast said to him is: "You have ripened already, and you are waiting to be brought in. Your exhaustion is a form of inner fermentation. You are beginning, ever so slowly to rot on the vine." (Whyte 2019) Through true and courageous conversations, we come to these ripe places, protected spaces, and the resonance of knowing what to do next.

In one group, a participant found herself in just such a ripe place, where she felt there was no opportunity because of two well-entrenched men in the department. Had she not hazarded herself to the conversation, she would not have realized she had given in to the situation at hand. Once she started to express herself, others who knew and valued her contributions were there to listen and talk it through with her. She decided to have a courageous conversation with her boss that left her concerned that she did the wrong thing. But it led to two other conversations that revealed her value to the organization. Several months later she had a promotion and the kinds of responsibilities that were commensurate to a person with her years of experience and capability.

I suggest to group participants that before they go to have the courageous conversation, or the fierce one, or the authentic one, before they go to "speak the truth with courage," as one client refers to it, they come back to some neutral emotional ground. In other words, do some reflecting and know what's been triggered in you, take back your projections and be open to learning something in the process. It helps to be sure that you know what your truth is. And to be willing to see a new truth. It could just be a defense, a justification, a complex, a dis-ease that is getting

> "Too frequently, what is sacred for a single individual is reduced to a prescriptive panacea for the many. What this overlooks is one simple fact: we heal as individual human beings. We have names, addresses and souls. What is good for one may be toxic to another."
>
> CARA BARKER,
> WORLD WEARY WOMEN

in the way of seeing things clearly and creating a real connection with another person.

In an instance where a male finance leader was ready to have a conversation he thought was courageous with a colleague he felt was taking credit for his work, he was stopped by his peer coach from the group. He had been practicing what he was going to say when this fellow participant thoughtfully asked if he might still be too angry to have the conversation. As they worked with this potential anger, it became clear to the finance leader that he was still feeling quite defensive. He recognized a pattern of being "slighted," which was fortunate for him, as had he not seen that pattern in the split second it appeared it would have been lost to his ego and various justifications. We talked it through privately, and he had another conversation with his peer coach before he had the conversation with his colleague. He reported that he was much more relaxed and nonjudgmental as a result of the preparatory conversations. He and his peer coach developed a trusting relationship in the process, and he was on his way to much better possibilities with his colleague. As Whyte reminds us, the conversation *is* the relationship. It is the work. If you can't hold a conversation with yourself as well as with others, you will have little success in the workplace or in any of your relationships.

> "Your inner emptiness conceals just as great a fullness, if only you would allow it to penetrate you."
>
> C. G. JUNG

Videoconference Groups

Being authentic and responsive in the moment can be somewhat awkward in Videoconference groups, where participants may come from multiple locations, even multiple countries. We've had colleagues from Germany, the U.K., Ireland, Brazil, and France connected into these meetings. It is best when individuals can coordinate business travel in order to join another group member in their conference room for the monthly meeting. This is even a good choice when individuals are in the same state but work in different locations. For example, a sales office and a manufacturing office might only be a relatively short distance from one another. If those participants share the responsibility for getting to the other location, it can make a big difference to their energy and engagement. They'll also have the ability to debrief personally with someone else in the group after the meeting rather than jump right back into work. Networking is a big positive outcome for group members, and I try to keep reminding them to take advantage of this time they have together. If relationships aren't developed, it is not likely participants will feel the same comfort in reconnecting later.

While much of the process remains the same in videoconference groups, there is an additional load on the facilitator to help individuals enter the conversation and not get lost in a corner of the screen. Those who are together in the headquarters office can easily forget to be inclusive of the others. The efforts they make in that direction, however, develop good practices for all meetings they're having via video.

HR Groups and Courageous Conversation

Having spent nearly 20 years working in HR organizations and another 15 working with them from the outside, I am always eager to continue my commitment to support their success.

In one large multinational organization, the HR group was having difficulty accepting the idea of using external coaches. We brought this into our group work and learned that it felt to them as if they were losing responsibilities to external resources. Using courageous conversations and developing vulnerability led the group members to clarify their own roles and better understand how to utilize external coaches. They had new insights and became more innovative in their support of their businesses. By the end, they were surprised that they had ever questioned the benefits of engaging external coaches. But that is what fear can do to us. When we don't have the courageous conversation in a safe environment, our fears hold us back.

While HR departments too often get a bad rap, bringing these individuals together in group sessions proves they have innovative ideas, dedication to collaborative working, and passion for their work. Watching them develop more sophistication in their leadership is exciting. When they invite some of their functional colleagues to join them, it not only breathes new life into their relationships but brings new levels of creativity to the system.

Organizational Life Cycle

Another aspect of group dynamics to consider arises from an organization's life cycle. Like humans who start in infancy, moving through toddler, childhood, adolescence, adult, and advanced age stages, organizations do the same. These stages are typically referred to as start-up, adolescent, mature, and decline. With group work we must consider where *this* particular organization is relative to life cycle in order to be prepared for the kinds of conversations that will come up or to prepare for those that we need to have. Organizations with a lot of longtime employees are quite different in their growth edges than start-ups. The courageous conversations and vulnerabilities vary. You need to know if you're supporting them in managing change or leading innovation.

Today there are so many interesting new organizations springing up and growing quickly it's hard to tell what stage they're in. Sometimes it requires doing some assessment conversations upfront with senior leaders beyond HR and a sponsor. The important thing is to have this on your radar when you're in the planning stages.

No matter the dynamics of the group or the organization, the work is based on the same fundamentals. Without some periods of reflection on our (facilitators' as well as participants') thoughts and feelings, without the opportunity for epiphanies, we remain unaware of the negative outcomes or lost opportunities of unconscious behavior. Those who commit themselves to the inner work are the beneficiaries of countless insights, enhanced relationships, and increased contentment—meaning they are less restless, *not* less driven. All who do this work are more able to accept their vulnerability, collaborate with others, and be more innovative. I don't know what emotions that brings about for you, but I do know that many participants seem to grow in their enthusiasm. It is as if they're starting a new job, full of the possibilities and joy that accompanies those first days. As to the benefits for you as the facilitator, well we'll talk more about that in the final chapter.

And, by the way, I do think we're talking about a deeper feeling than happiness. Earlier (Part II, Chapter One), I noted that happiness might not be enough. One individual had prioritized *Happiness* as her last value in the list of 21 on her VAL® report. She initially took a beating from her colleagues: "How could you not value happiness, what's wrong with you? Are you depressed? Are you an alien from another planet?" She didn't know how to respond right away as it even sounded weird to her. She was challenged, she was taking risks and learning. She was developing strong collaborations and a balanced team. She was very content in many ways, yet still driven to achieve more. "Happy" just didn't seem to measure up to what she felt. She used words like "fulfilled," "enthusiastic," and "energized." Her team members came around because they knew her and would have said she was a happy person, but they realized that for her *happiness* seemed too trite an idea.

> "The happiness metric is a poor measure of a life. Happiness that is in any way based on denial, distraction, or ignorance is an affront to the soul and its depth."
>
> JAMES HOLLIS AS HEARD ON *SPEAKING OF JUNG*, PODCAST #25.

There is a lot we can learn from gathering together in small groups and learning to be vulnerable, curious, open, and more fully engaged. There are many courageous conversations to be had in helping us work toward more wholeheartedness in our workplaces. Isn't that really what we're after when we look to increase employee engagement—certainly a hot topic over the last decade?

Questions to consider

How do you define happiness?

What enables your vulnerability in your work?

Have you witnessed others developing their vulnerability or becoming more whole-hearted in your work with them? What does that look like? How does it impact them and their environment?

How do you want to support greater employee engagement in the organizations that you consult to?

IV

What Organizations and Participants Say About Their Group Experience

"Gratitude is not a mere word; it is not a mere concept. It is the living breath of your real existence on earth."

Sri Chinmoy

By now, you likely have some thoughts about the benefits of group work in organizations. I have seen firsthand how people respond and grow through this experience. Our last two sessions bring opportunities for the participants to express this growth and share the value they gained from their faithful involvement. In this chapter I will review the organizational benefits of group work as well as the individual benefits as expressed by actual participants.

HR, sponsors, and senior leadership are quick to note the organizational value. They are grateful to bring coaching to more of their leaders at a much-reduced rate to that of individual coaching engagements. They see how relationships are enhanced and networks are created through stronger communication skills and greater confidence. They experience a new level of executive presence as demonstrated by participants' character, substance, and style[1]. They recognize more emotional strength and greater resilience in the individuals. When these leaders sit in on 30 minutes of our last session, they tend to be complimentary and quick to share

---

1   Character, substance, and style as per Bates' model of executive presence.

what they've been seeing transpire in their employees. Renewed energy, accountability, and creativity are often cited. There's a nice sense of pride in the room from both sides.

As the facilitator, I want the moment to last as long as possible, as I know that all too soon, new challenges will be upon the participants and they could forget what they accomplished. They, too, want to hold onto this feeling as long as they can.

Supporting Employee Wellness and Engagement

Take a look back at Chapter One in Part One, under the headline of "Coaching," and let's revisit the stages of analytical engagement: encounter, revelation, intimacy, interpenetration, combination, death of limited personal consciousness, and emergence of more whole, authentic consciousness. Is this not what we hear in these comments? Through group work, you support your organizations in so much that is fundamental to making people well—mentally sharp and engaged. Trust and rapport are high. There's a new level of connectedness from the practice of letting down their guard with one another, being vulnerable, listening more intently. And interestingly enough, the Types® have not formed cliques in the end. They often start out with some comfort in sitting or chatting with others of the same Type®, but because they are partnered with different Types® for their peer coaching, they are pushed into relationships that are more diverse.

In one women's group, two off-site women, one from Project Management and another from Manufacturing, made a strong connection with a woman in Finance. They used the opportunity to learn more about how the budgeting process worked and to get a better understanding of the company's financial systems. And the woman from Finance gained a new understanding of how her decisions impacted the employees in

"Our privilege and responsibility as servants of the healing arts is to create an environment, provide a method, and inspire people to touch what we, beyond any evidence to the contrary, know is who they really are because we have touched this within ourselves."

SAKI SANTORELLI

various locations. Having spent time on learning to be curious (Tables 2 & 3) they, psychologically speaking, "interpenetrated" one another. This deeper sharing changed their perspectives about how they did their work. The larger impact, the meaningful impression, may have even altered their worldview. Referred to as a *metanoia*, this fundamental shift in seeing is the kind of growth and maturity we need to move beyond mere economic gains to human well-being.

The Final Day = A New Beginning

Participants quickly jump to certain questions in our final meeting: How will I maintain this new level of confidence? How can I keep up with peer coaching sessions with my colleagues? Now that I don't have to report my insights back to anyone, will I still recognize them? How will I continue my reading of leadership literature? We work with these questions after their leaders leave and we get to the final details of closing out the group. But while they are still together, participants often share what they feel they have individually gleaned from the intensive. Some will talk about communication skills they've developed or enhanced strategic and big-picture perspectives. Most feel they know themselves much better and have a language for expressing that knowledge. They are more aware of their strengths, interests, shortcomings, and triggers, and not afraid to say it. They are willing to laugh at themselves and nudge one another with that intimate knowing of where the other has evolved over the months. They talk of knowing how to get more support for what they need, having more confidence in themselves, and having a better understanding of what it means to be a leader. Someone typically mentions feeling more agile—more able to respond to the pressures and changes that are so constant. In one session a woman spoke of the ability to stop spending so much time on the endless recycling of frustration, anger, and bitterness. No one wants to use the word, but I often see a new level of maturity and know that they will benefit greatly from that.

Usually, either one of the leaders or one of the participants demonstrates a new rapport that has developed between them. For example, in one group a leader playfully said, "Well, now I see how I'm in the trouble I'm in; she now knows how to get what she needs from me." In another group a male participant kindly noted that he had a new appreciation for his female boss's challenges and her ability to handle her male colleagues. He said he hoped he would prove to be a better colleague to the females he worked with and felt he was making strides there. His manager was quick to say he was having success and enjoying many more collaborations in his work. Remember kinship libido? This is it.

When the managers take their exit and it is just "us" in the room again, there is a new level of delight and lightheartedness. They're done. They've accomplished this big thing. They see their transformation. Then some will sigh and note their disappointment in knowing they won't meet next month. And that's when they begin to make commitments to one another about quarterly catchups, lunches, visits, and such. Some organizations start having reunions so groups get to meet up and learn who else has been through this transformational experience. In one organization, after our third women's group, the female CEO teamed up with me to have a social evening and "fireside chat," with the three groups coming together for the first time. Afterward, I had many comments from the women about their feeling valued and what a great experience it was to have that kind of intimate time with the CEO.

Regrets & Commitments

In one of the last two meetings, I typically ask participants if there is anything anyone wishes they had done differently, more of, or less of in the process. The answers always include: "I wish I would have gotten more into the journaling" or "I wish I would have taken more advantage of time with my peer coaches." They typically express hope that they will keep up with some leadership reading. And they frequently express a new confidence that they can be in that conversation when someone says, "We need more leadership on this project or this issue."

One of the last questions I ask is: "What do you want to work on now, or is there a question driving your next developmental experience?" Now that they've effectively made a commitment to their development, I want to see them continue that with some fidelity. Those hours will get absorbed so quickly—they know it and I know it, so if they can agree to guard even an hour a month before they leave the room, they're more likely to follow through.

For some, there are promises of sharing experiences, stories and articles, and visiting when they're abroad, but there is typically someone who makes a really big commitment, e.g., to do their MBA, to speak at a conference, or to say "yes" to a project lead role. Additionally important are the commitments to say "no" to an offer or even pull out of something because they know it would suck the life out of them, or it would put them on the wrong track. This, too, is how we ensure engagement in our organizations. It is how an organization wins the *war for talent* we spoke of early in the book.

Group time provides the opportunity to claim the keys to one's own "happiness," joy, success, and contentment by working on the inside and seeing how that impacts their outer world. It is a time when participants learn to observe and notice what is happening in the moment, experiencing "now" without judgment. And through these observations, in time, they can watch those patterns that have held them hostage slip away.

Now, of course, is the bigger challenge of sustaining the insights, ahas, and commitments. We trust we've laid some of the necessary groundwork along the way to ensure a good measure of this. Now it's up to the individual and the organization to follow through. The individual has to keep up his or her own work, and the organization has to be a good shepherd. The manager and HR have some responsibility for following up and reinforcing, supporting, encouraging, challenging, and listening in order to get the most from and for each employee.

Questions to consider

Where do you feel most comfortable with your skills and ability to begin or enhance your facilitation of groups?

What concerns do you have?

What commitments do you want to make to your own further development? Why?

What is key to your "happiness," joy, success?

Part III

Five Key Challenges (or Opportunities) in Group Coaching

"When we release expectation and experience appreciation, all the moments of our lives become openings and opportunities."

KRISTI NELSON,
EXECUTIVE DIRECTOR, GRATEFULNESS.ORG

Introduction

If you've read my earlier books, you'll know that I have found poetry to be very useful to gaining self-awareness and insight. Recently I fell for a poem called "Because Even the Word Obstacle is an Obstacle" by Alison Luterman. Not only do I love it as a swimmer for the many references to the experience of pool life but also because it causes me to reconsider the idea of obstacles and challenges. Luterman starts her poem this way: "Try to love everything that gets in your way."

For participants joining a group, there are potentially many obstacles. The time commitment is first and foremost and includes the meeting time, the time with peer coaches, the reading and reflection time, and the prep time. It can be very hard for individuals to cut further into both work and family time. There is also the obstacle of opening one's self up to learning and personal insight and the vulnerability we spoke of earlier. There might be obstacles relative to boss and coworker support. All of these can challenge someone's choice in wanting to commit to group work. And yet, for those who do take the challenge, it seems to be with a mindset of "opportunity."

In response to my asking, "Is this a good time for you to participate in the group?" one very busy executive and mother with a newly diagnosed bipolar teen said, "I might never get a chance like this again." Then she added, "And I can't believe that I was invited out of all the possible other women I know." She said she was eager to learn more about how she could demonstrate and extend her leadership. She didn't look at the group work as an obstacle but as an opportunity.

Challenges for those designing a group process might include deciding who the 10 participants should be, if the organization is ready, and if the leadership is ready. Does the organization know what competencies and capabilities it wants to build in its leadership? Do the organization's leaders know the future they're working toward? Will there be international growth, leadership growth, technological growth, product development?

It is a tall order to "love everything that gets in your way," but try it for just a day. It's a great challenge that yields a lot of opportunity or at least greater possibility. It's a glass-half-full approach, but it is not naïve optimism. Luterman concludes the poem by noting, "Your impatience must bow in service to the larger story, because if something is in your way, it is going your way, the way of all beings: toward darkness, toward light." Our challenges and our suffering move us in the direction of insight, new life, and energy. They bring us greater awareness and a more mature level of cooperation—defenses drop, personal neediness becomes less important, we see the value of others, and the *larger story*, and we are transformed.

In this section we will review the five key challenges of the group process and show how obstacles are often opportunities that can lead to our transformation.

I

Choosing the Right Participants

"We are all linked by a fabric of unseen connections.
This fabric is constantly changing and evolving. This field
is directly structured and influenced by our behavior
and by our understanding."

David Bohm

Perhaps the real question is: Is there a "right" participant? I think we can get as close to *right* as possible by knowing the organization's goals and what it wants to see more of from its leaders. What does the organization feel it needs from its leadership, now and into the next decade? In response to talent management needs in organizations, Insight Group Work targets high potentials and emerging talent. Sometimes organizations want to give an opportunity to those thought of as *hidden* talent. These individuals have shown that they have a good bit to offer, but they haven't been tested or they have not had the opportunity to exhibit their capability widely.

The other way to look at this question is to consider who would be the *wrong* participants. On first thought, we might say a person who is impatient might not be a good fit, or a person who is a bit of a narcissist might not work, or someone who talks a lot or not enough might impede the process—and, well, all of these could be true. But any of these qualities mixed with high potential—meaning strong manager of people, the right experiences, curious, or smart and agile—could make the person a very good candidate. There are no crystal balls. A group that looks "perfect" might not have the mix of personalities or styles that can bring out edgy or rigorous questions and step out of the good and politically correct persona.

It is good to find an interesting mix, a diverse group of people who are ready for a developmental experience. Ideally, HR works across its network in the various businesses in the organization to facilitate good participant choices. When a sponsor is chosen from the business as a resource to the group, he or she is usually part of the discussions to determine the group members, which contributes to a good diversity of candidates. Some organizations will have an application process to learn why individuals might want to be a part of such a process. This can also flesh out those who, while they might be interested, are just not right at that time because of other distractions and commitments. Those who speak of goals and aspirations and show some self-awareness and an interest in learning tend to stand out. There is a saying in OD and large-scale group work, and I think it applies here, that "the right people will be in the room." This means that with a certain amount of planning and intentionality up front, at some point we have to trust what has brought this group together at this time.

Making Intentional Choices

In one organization, the HR leader was struggling with a potential participant put forth by an R&D leader. This individual was thought of as low energy and a bit negative. Yet, others marveled at his brilliance and capacity for work. The HR leader worried that he might bring down the group. She was concerned that he might be good in his current position but lack the ability to get to the next level and therefore was not the right fit. In the end, we decided to take a chance because of the manager's urging. He saw someone full of potential with a need to develop relationally. It turned out to be a good decision. While this participant wasn't gregarious by any means, he made good contributions and clearly developed in his ability to relate with others. It's good to remember that a certain lowness that shows up in an individual can be circumstantial and short-term. We all have highs and lows. And, some live on one end more than the other. The more conscious we are of both experiences, the more we can learn from them and find ways to be effective. I have worked with people who have shared that they struggle with depression, an eating disorder or ADD. They were all consciously managing these issues and had coping strategies.

> "The sort of depression we most commonly think of when we use the word depression…is a manifestation of the autonomy of the psyche. The ego, the conscious sense of who we are, wishes to invest energy in a certain direction, perhaps in service to economic goals, but the soul has another agenda. It autonomously withdraws the invested energy, inverts it, and as it withdraws into the psyche it often pulls the ego in after it." (Hollis 2005)

This, of course, is not referring to clinical depression. The individual who may be in the wrong job or taking on too much may be experiencing a situational or temporary depression. Such misalignments or overwhelming circumstances are often seen more clearly in the group work. In this way, a process that is whole-person-centered can help someone who has a lot of capability see and make the adjustments that can further strengthen their resilience and effectiveness. It can encourage such people to seek change or help. They can strategize and develop a network that helps support them over time. And, Hollis suggests, people who think they're highly skilled at their work but don't find it very satisfying may come to see that as "idolatry" and be able to make meaningful adjustments. They may be investing energy in the wrong place and satisfying the ego's needs but not the soul's. This typically ends badly or at least abruptly. Employees who are most engaged are energized because they are moved by their work.

Conscious Consideration of Participant Alignments and Differences

While there could be two and even three generations in a group, we want to be mindful of how this will impact participants—especially those on either end of the continuum. Jung differentiates between the first half of life and the second half of life, which can be a more useful guide. This is not an age but a mindset. Those in the first half of life are in the establishment phase, ensuring they have the knowledge and resources to meet their personal and professional goals. During that period we can eschew certain values and ignore the cost. But once the basic goals are met and there is a natural curiosity about something more—a life with greater meaning—we are called to live differently. This meaning-making phase doesn't come on overnight, although sometimes it might feel that way. It is a gradual interest in and concern about ideas and work that align with a person's long-term values, interests, and criteria for integrity. As Hollis' quote above notes, the soul is making its desires known, which will cause some disequilibrium. If a majority of the group members are moving into this "second half of life," they will be bored with the conversations of those at the earlier phase. And this is a population that it behooves organizations to learn how to support. They have knowledge, experience, history, and maturity.

> Wholly unprepared, they embark upon the second half of life. Or, are there perhaps colleges for forty-year olds which prepare them for their coming life and its demands as the ordinary colleges introduce our young people to knowledge of the world? No, thoroughly unprepared we take the step into the afternoon of life; worse still, we take this step with the false assumption that our truth and ideals will serve us as hitherto. But we cannot live the afternoon of life according to the programme of life's morning; for what was great in the morning will be little at evening, and what in the morning was true will at evening have become a lie. (Jung 1960)

I think that group work can serve very nicely as a "college for 40-year-olds," preparing participants for the second half of life—although we can hold that to the one-to-one sessions if it applies to just a couple of participants.

The mixes of ages and generations in a group have value for networking—engaging with those who are thinking differently—and can offer some mentorship or knowledge transfer that might not happen otherwise. It can be a detriment to the group experience when first-half-of-lifers and second-half-of-lifers are frustrated with each other because of their differing needs. For example, while first-half-of-lifers might be focused on the next promotion, second-half-of-lifers may want to know how one can stay relevant in their work and committed to their individuation and the creative expression that might not fit their current organizational lives. They might gain value from discussing what retirement or semiretirement might look like and creating multiyear plans for effective transitioning. This might sound like the antithesis of what an organization might want in a leader development process. In actuality, it can enhance engagement a great deal as employees aren't distracted by the confusion they might be feeling about their commitment to their work versus that of a meaningful life. It can also help organizations that want to see people transition effectively but are often pushed to let people go who have seemingly aged out of a high-driving leadership style. Of course, they would never use the "age" word, but that in itself hides a potential opportunity for mutually beneficial outcomes.

Every mix of participants offers opportunities and challenges. It is important to find those opportunities and increase the outcomes in service to the individuals and the organizational needs and goals.

Questions to consider

What is your natural approach to dealing with obstacles?

What are some of the challenges that you have experienced or are anticipating in group work?

Can you see opportunity in those challenges?

II

Sponsors, Mentors and Speakers

"The more clearly you can state your expectations, the better you will be able to plan and the more meaningful the experience will be for the participants. A lack of careful thought and planning will show up later in a variety of problems that lead to confusion and floundering among the participants."

MARIANNE SCHNEIDER COREY AND GERALD COREY

Any and all "extras" can be added distraction, confusion, and challenge, or they can bring new opportunities for learning and growth. In most cases, they likely land somewhere in the middle. As soon as others start to play in the group sandbox, you potentially dilute the effort you have so carefully designed. You lose the safety of the container that allows for the deeper transformative work. Let's look at the various ways this can play out.

Sponsors

Sponsors are often chosen from the business to add a bit of legitimacy or credibility to a new organizational effort, such as group coaching. They can be very helpful in thinking about what is important right now in the business and they can have foresight that may not be as available to the HR team. I enjoy the challenges they often present in the planning stage. Some have helped enormously in the choosing of participants.

But after that, there can be relatively little for them to do. On some occasions, however, sponsors stepped up throughout the process. In one example, the sponsor went out of his way to make himself available to individuals and also provided funds for the global group to come to the U.S. headquarters so they could all meet together in one space. None of us could have guessed he would contribute in this way and that it was going to be so important to this particular group.

In another instance a very senior, highly experienced woman sponsored two women's groups. Several of the participants had formerly been mentored by her, and all had a high level of respect and admiration for her work. Her standing in the organization lent a level of integrity and value that would have been hard to duplicate. When you're introducing a process like Insight Group Coaching, that isn't as tangible and easily described as training programs are, this can be a huge benefit. People just trust it is going to be worth their involvement.

On the negative side, sponsors can get too involved in the process by supporting favorites or having strong suggestions about books and ideas for sessions. They can be too focused on having an impact and insert themselves to a degree that takes away from the transformational aspects of the group work. So, when you're deciding on a sponsor, it is important to clearly outline the parameters of the role with the HR leader (or other lead contact) and make sure the person chosen will have the right sensibility for the position. In one instance where I had an energetic, highly interested sponsor who had way too many ideas for how we could run the group, we met the challenge by giving her a specific task to focus on where she would have the highest impact and a clear raison d'être. She did a great job on the added activity and everyone felt good about the outcome.

Mentors

While I am often asked about the use of mentors to support participants, I have yet to incorporate them in the group initiatives. There are several reasons for this. First, without explanations that often require a great deal of time and effort, they may not be considerate of the context of how life is different for their mentee. They also may not know how varied leadership styles can be. Mentors typically share information and knowledge from their own leadership style and experiences. While they have had successes—which I don't mean to downplay—they are not necessarily experts on leadership, and rarely on human development. Additionally, mentors can be directive and have strong opinions, and they likely will not realize why group participants are not being told how to be leaders. The participants are learning to give and get peer coaching, and they are getting one-on-one coaching from the group facilitator. That is typically enough to manage along with feedback from their bosses and potential conversations with HR and the group sponsor, never mind all of the other aspects of group work.

Many of the participants have enjoyed the benefits of mentors over the years. Those who haven't experienced such relationships come to understand their value through group discussions and are encouraged to find mentors. Sometimes that happens during the year of group work but often it is a focus after the group work is complete.

To make mentorship a part of the initiative it would require training so that mentors could reinforce the messages that are most important and aligned with the process. To truly be in synch, it would be best if they went through a group themselves. If we did go this route, we still would have to be content knowing there will be some who push another agenda, and share strong opinions on their own ideas of leadership. While there can certainly be value to their ideas, they can bring another level of complexity that may only add confusion and not serve the process. As it is, in the early months some participants would rather we just told them what leadership is and is not and get on with it. We are asking them to hold out on hard and fast answers, rules and musts, and wallow through the uncertainty, complexity and inescapable ambiguity. By contrast, mentors are typically trying to resolve confusion and uncertain situations and provide logical answers. Work life requires both capabilities, and group work strives to develop this kind of agility.

Speakers

One of my best group experiences as a participant was with a group that featured a lot of outside speakers. It also happened to be the one where we met for two to three days at a time over the course of 15 months. We had the time to have speakers and debrief their contributions, integrating them with other work we were doing before having another speaker. Those speakers were carefully chosen and prepped for their talks. While speakers can be valuable contributors, with the streamlined process of Insight Group Coaching, where we are trying to get a robust, transformative experience in the least time possible, we find it best not to have them.

Typically, organizations have other opportunities to invite speakers to meet with the leadership whether through employee networks, town halls or special events. These can be experiential, entertaining, and engaging. Often the attendees enjoy hearing how others have learned the business, developed their reputations, and found success, but it may have little to do with how they would best do those things. A speaker dropped into the already tight time frame breaks the flow, development, and understanding of the group work.

In one situation where I was pressed to add a speaker (and truly wanted to be open to the possibilities of what might come out of the experience), I became aware in the session that the individual was already overused in the organization and had relatively little new to offer. He was very enthusiastic and had a fairly quick career progression but didn't represent the maturity or message that aligned with the work we were doing. The group members were impressed that he took time to speak with them, but his talk added nothing more than an ego boost.

If we could ever increase the current two-hour sessions to three hours, then having a couple of appropriate, well-prepared speakers may be quite useful. It would require a strategic approach and time to debrief and make use of the information and experience. But there is great value in the bit of pressure to accomplish goals within the timeframe of just nine two-hour meetings. It gently pushes people off the ledge of comfort and gets them experimenting without too much deliberation.

This brings me to one last notation on this subject—the most important one—before we move on. We must realize that all of these efforts—sponsors, mentors, speakers—are outward focusing, and the work of Insight Group Coaching is focused on the pause, the reflection, and the growth and insight of the individual. The point is to get some time to go inward so that when participants are called outward they can be at their best and enjoy their authenticity.

Questions to consider

Do you have experience with sponsors, mentors and/or speakers that would make you want to include them in your group work?

Would that work well with your philosophy, methodology and goals?

Extreme Organizational Change

"As you set out for Ithaka hope your road is a long one,
full of adventure, full of discovery."

C. P. Cavafy

When organizations are going through a lot of change, it might drive leaders to resist any seemingly unnecessary initiatives. That could make sense. Yet, the group can help stabilize and strengthen leaders for the baffling and disorienting times they're going through. I will share stories from two groups I led where organizations were experiencing extreme organizational change. This created a great deal of noise and distraction. But the opportunity to come together in small reflective groups helped individuals to make the most of these stressful and troubling times and to build skills to support their teams through them as well.

In the first example, I led eight mixed male/female groups with the organization that ranged from new director level to senior vice president. This appeared to be a well-run organization with a great deal of success. The employees were unusually happy and by all outward measures seemed to enjoy their work and the majority of their colleagues. But as they say, all good things must come to an end, and so it was here. A new president came on board with two groups still in process. He was quick to invalidate the collegial, relational approach employees had to their work and shift the attention to "producing." Most of my contacts through my group work or one-on-one executive coaching came to feel that they were meant to be preparing the company for sale—a relatively unspoken but ubiquitous feeling. A significant number of employees bailed in the first six to 10 months, adding to the anxiety of those left behind. The challenges that arose daily led to more one-on-one coaching and supporting individuals to find their way in the new normal. But the new normal never lasted very long, and it felt like an exercise in futility for many. The value for the groups in process at the time of the upheaval was that they had others they could try to make sense of things with, allies. The group turned into every bit as much a support group as a leadership development opportunity. The participants learned things about leadership that they certainly would not have had this transition not occurred, but they also learned about resilience in a way they couldn't have understood in the old paradigm. They learned how to pivot on a moment's notice and how to have agility relationally and cognitively as well as behaviorally. Some learned to have tolerance for ambiguity and *take* leadership in spite of not having any clear direction. And in the end, all of the participants gained a network, greater confidence, and the ability to make tough decisions. For some, that meant staying around and supporting this next iteration of the organization for as long as they could; for others, it meant finding a better fit for their next period of growth and development.

In the second situation, I worked with an organization that had a lot of long-term employees working hard and doing good work. But doing good work was no longer good enough. The organization was behind technologically, and government regulations and new standards of operation were pressuring it to make quick and big change. A new president and CEO took the helm, the first female in that role. I had conversations with several of the "old guard male leaders" to guide them in, first, accepting this new leader and then embracing her. She had been in our first women's group some years earlier, and a few years after, I had taken her to see David Whyte speak, which she very much enjoyed. Having interacted in these ways, I felt I knew her well enough to support her with confidence.

She championed two more women's groups during this time of great transformation in the organization. But it was a wild time. There were continuous announcements of leadership changes and restructurings, new roles and new ideas. Most people were antsy, to say the least. They were also confused and having difficulty explaining to the next level of management what was going on, why they shouldn't be anxious, and how they could encourage their direct reports. Both women's groups were highly engaged as they sought answers, guidance, and motivation to stay the course. They were challenging to facilitate as energy was bouncing in every direction and it vacillated between good and bad thoughts, feelings, and emotions. Sometimes it was best to just let them talk it out, *feel* the commonality among them (step away from *industry and intensity* for just a moment) and see them come around to how they would go boldly—or even haltingly—forward.

As a "Feeling" Type®, I did have compassion and empathy for them. But I also found that I had to consciously move toward "Thinking" and creating balance and facilitating an objective response. We often came back to goals, even when they didn't feel sure of what they were, or especially then, as they needed to create some order, stay grounded, and support the next level down. We shifted complaints to useful critique in order to get to legitimate objectives. The participants came up with ideas on how to direct others and manage their own anxiety so they could temper the turbulence and make good decisions. And I think it's safe to say that they left the group feeling better than when they came in each month. They all agreed with one woman who said, "I feel so much better when I see one of you in a meeting." Just the sight of someone they had built trust and camaraderie with—kinship—made their work more tolerable and gave them more confidence.

The following winter, the president sponsored a reunion of all previous women's groups' participants, and I facilitated a Q&A with her that helped to unify them and their experiences. She was so adept at communication—providing information, challenging with what-ifs and possibilities, and supporting by noting many of the wonderful accomplishments they were all a part of leading—that it really was a very positive experience. The women left buoyed up in a way they hadn't felt in some time.

Many individuals make up an organization. They are all in varying stages of development and life. When an organization is going through a great deal of change, it is like sand shifting underneath the employees' feet. So, even the ones who are fairly stable feel the discomfort of not knowing what tomorrow will bring. Our work in the group offers participants the chance to build their resilience in order to bring some stability wherever they can. This resilience comes with greater self-awareness. If we come back to Jung's main idea relative to personality development, we are always working toward *individuation*. We are always finding "true north" for ourselves—for the Self. The good and the bad, the beautiful and the scary, the true and the questionable all come together to challenge us to what we will be. How will we respond to what life brings our way? What growth will come from the hardships? How might we support others as they are knocked off balance by unanticipated changes?

> "Ultimately, work on self is inseparable from work in the world. Each mirrors the other; each is a vehicle for the other. When we change ourselves, our values and actions change as well."
>
> CHARLES EISENSTEIN

We are always fabricating ourselves—pulling the threads into some new thing, creating our own myth. "Ithika"[1] is home, but it is the adventure and the challenges that make the hero—or prepare the mature, grounded executive. And those experiences will have a somewhat different impact on all of us. "This is the task of individuation: to differentiate ourselves from the herd and take what is discovered and put it to use for the greater good, in practical ways. Paradoxically, by becoming aware of what makes us unique, we discover our connection (Barker 2001)."

"What will you do with your one wild and precious life?" Mary Oliver asks in a poem called *Summer's Day*. It's important to ask ourselves this always, to find ways to step into our true selves, creating new possibilities and opportunities from old challenges and difficulties.

---

1   Referring to the journey of Odysseus. Poem by C. P. Cavafy that I encourage you to read.

Questions to consider

Have you experienced extreme organizational change? Note some examples and what you learned from it.

Do you have the skills and experience, and would you enjoy supporting others through extreme change?

What further training or development would you seek for success with this type of work?

IV

Being the Facilitator Doesn't Mean You're in Control

"Be a lamp or a lifeboat or a ladder. Help someone's soul heal. Walk out of your house like a shepherd."

RUMI

Perhaps a shepherd is a good metaphor for the work of the group facilitator and coach. There is the appearance of control in the shepherd's work, and yet things happen: A sheep gets separated from the flock, gets caught between some rocks, gets anxious and scared. Reacting to his circumstances, all manner of problems are possible. When we are shepherding a group, we are indeed trying to keep the flock together and yet not so tightly together they can't get fed in their own individual way.

The group needs different voices to express different paths, approaches, and ideas in order to stay interesting. The loose-tight approach of Insight Group Coaching is meant to enable that which is most important in the moment. So, while the facilitator should be ready for a shift in topic or ideas, we are not necessarily ready for *anything* that might come up. Sometimes it has value to speak up when we're taken off guard or distracted by a member's behavior (e.g., texting, having continuous sidebar conversations, etc.), but other times we choose to let something play out or we don't choose—it seems to choose on its own. Sometimes we cringe at a comment but decide to let it go. Or, we hold our breath to see what happens next as we think we might have made a mistake in judgment. Managing every moment for perfection would result in boredom and seriously curtail learning, especially the deeper learning we're looking for.

In one group, I did think I made a mistake—I thought I provoked a participant too quickly when I challenged a request she made. It felt as if she was pushing an unnecessary point. Later, I was reminded that if you work on being conscious, if you stay in learner mode, you can't really make a mistake. Maybe it had been too early, maybe it would have been "better" if I waited until she felt more secure. But maybe that would have been too late. Maybe she would have been lulled into a false belief that she was indeed perfectly right in her expectations of leadership and what seemed like the need to get her own way. Sometimes we have to make our best guess in seconds. Those teachable moments don't get served up on a silver platter in every two-hour monthly meeting. And yet, if we do our side of the work, paying attention to the alignment of personality and values with the behaviors and talk of the individuals, we find many opportunities to inquire and broaden participants' thinking. As we discussed in depth in *The Golden Key*, attunement is very germane to our effectiveness.

The teachable moment may come from a seemingly innocuous statement or a complex challenge. Sometimes there is an unconscious beckoning in the group to speak to a certain dilemma, issue, or ideology. We must always be listening.

All too often, especially in the first sessions, participants are rather conservative and careful. The last thing you want to do is stifle new ideas or out-of-the-ordinary kinds of approaches by being too quick to challenge. Providing safety and managing to confidentiality rules enables vulnerability to come more easily. There are guidelines for the work, as you've read in previous chapters, but there are very few rules, leaving the facilitator open to more potential messiness. Craig and Patricia Neal note: "We have found that to bring authentic engagement to our gatherings, it is helpful to *intend* to have authentic engagement. This one intention, or awareness, can sometimes hold a group together (Neal 2011)." In the opening meeting, I offer several intentions of this kind—sometimes folded into my comments and other times more directly. Overall, the readings and responsibilities provide the intention for the session, but occasionally I will note other intentions. For example, I might say, "It's my intention that we get into discussing what is working particularly well for you and where you may be having difficulty integrating these new ideas with your daily activities." This sets a direction for individuals to step into a defined yet open space. It appreciates that there may be challenges. Finally, it also provides an example to them of options in running their meetings.

One of our core books, *Leadership and Self-Deception,* tends to come up repeatedly as participants set the intention for catching how they deceive themselves and how they can make their lives easier through awareness. Sometimes an individual will get close to what appears to be an important insight (introduced by the archetypal Self, from the unconscious) but will quickly justify why a certain thing happened. The participant actually gets hijacked by the ego, which wants to stay in control at all cost. At times, a group member, often the person's peer coach, might attempt to resurrect the insight in a very kind and supportive way. But most times it isn't quite the same, as the ego has gained ground and is striving to stay aligned with the persona. In that moment the opportunity may be lost, but a certain tension and inner conflict remain.

> Only a few people will consciously accept the responsibility for the process that their life is undergoing. They live it or are lived by it or are simply driven by it, instead of experiencing it. When the unconscious demands consciousness, then there is always much praised goodwill and common sense that enables us to deny it and to boast about our willpower. The breakthrough is thus "successfully" foiled. — C.A. Meier

Of course, this happens daily, and through our work, we are hoping that it will happen less often and that the Self, as the center of energy and the inner guide, will gain some wins. Just one or two keen insights can be invaluable—noting an inflation or attitude of grandiosity, for example. Jung warned that "every experience of the Self is a defeat for the ego (Jung 1963)." This means that the ego gets humbled, and the individual may feel some awkwardness or embarrassment. No matter what, it is important for the facilitator to "hold the space" and support the individual or group by not judging what has happened or trying to push a point. It is not our job to fix anyone. When the time is right, the lesson will be brought home. Likewise, if something does come up that may be upsetting or disturbing to a participant or the group, it is up to the facilitator to "manage the container." This means that we create safety and security. In some cases, you will ask the group, "Can we agree that this stays in this room?" Then you go around and look at each person, getting a nod of agreement. In one situation where an individual gave some upsetting information to the group, I asked her, "Would you like this to be kept confidential?" I assumed the answer would be yes, but I wanted her to be able to set the expectation.

At times being a coach means being patient with a client's repetitive stories just as a therapist or analyst would be. When under stress and triggered, clients will often retell the same series of events. That is often how one works through confusing or stuck places. If a coach insinuates that a person should get over it and move on in order to get control of the situation, he is just caught up in the patriarchal nightmare that already exists in excess, discouraging vulnerability and a little messiness. If you cover up what is genuine, you prolong the opportunity for growth. You keep the person in a childlike state—well-behaved and obedient. Listening to the message beneath the words and guiding individuals to hear what they are actually expressing will enable you both to find your way through the ambiguous, often repetitive muddle.

Letting Go

By the time you are reaching the end of a group, there might be the desire to tie it all up with a neat bow. Yet, there may still be obstacles to overcome without overly controlling the process. It seems inevitable that in the last meeting someone tries to come up with a plan to keep it going just as is (minus the facilitator). Others tend to jump in to challenge, realizing that this isn't sustainable without support. In one situation, a group did decide it would keep it going in spite of my gentle inquiries and challenge. It wouldn't be right for me to tell the members they couldn't do it if that is what they really wanted to do, but I also felt quite sure they didn't know what kind of work was involved in trying to manage it themselves. In this one instance, they did go away with a clear plan for continuing and incorporated a *giveback* aspect. The giveback entailed each of them bringing another woman with them each month so more could benefit as they did. I voiced my concerns that perhaps it was too often or would be too many people. They assured me they wanted to do it and they would rotate responsibility, making it very easy. As far as the size goes, they said it wouldn't be as intimate, but they could extend their reach, and it would have a different value. I did have to love their enthusiasm. But as you might imagine, that was the extent of it—a lot of enthusiasm and good intent, but too much work to organize and execute. They never did get the plan off the ground. The affirming part was that I felt I must have really made it look very easy.

Co-Creation

The leader of the group is a facilitator, a convener, and a coach. As a facilitator, one tries to make things happen, to clear a way for things to happen. A convener has the role of "gathering and 'holding' people, in a safe and generative space, for the sake of authentic engagement (Neal 2011)." And as a coach, I am supporting the individual and the group in their efforts whether they need *a lamp* to elucidate some new feeling or idea, *a lifeboat* when they're drowning with possibilities, ego or vulnerability, or *a ladder* as they climb to new heights with new job opportunities, expansion, or thoughts and strategy.

You've heard some of my stories about participants trying to take control in certain circumstances. That will happen. But too much control in response is not a good thing. Having the opportunity and the preparedness for responding in a collaborative way on an issue is part of the work. Co-creating a way forward demonstrates the ability to work effectively with others. It's not usually about my way or their way, but the patience to allow a third way to appear. A new way.

Managing Oneself

The second book in this series, *Authenticity as an Executive Coach*, is all about self-management. In it, I offer a list of questions for the coach's reflection. These questions are great for after group sessions as well. We might ask:

What expectations did I have for today's session?

What expectations did I have for the group participants?

What happened between me and the group today?

What kept me from saying what I wanted to say?

What does my imagination or reverie tell me about this group?[1]

Our journaling from these reflections gives us new insights and opportunities for more consciousness and greater wisdom in working with the group. It may also give us direction for ideas or information that needs reframing, repeating or reinforcing. Finally, it allows us to model the value of reflection and journaling for the group in hopes that participants will be more likely to give it a try.

In the process of reflection, we may come up against our own anxiety or frustration, for it can seem like little is happening for a long time. Some participants appear to make very little progress as their insights don't come within our process period. But they will come in the years ahead. People have told me of articles or books they reread (or finally get to reading) sometime later, and there is a resonance that stimulates insights or inquiries that lead to new growth and enlargement long after our meetings are finished. Once again, this speaks to our lack of control in the sessions. And, of course, control should not be what we're after. Transformational work comes out of the messiness.

---

1   Questions originally taken from the work of Jungian Analyst, Mel Marshak.

Questions to consider

Are you comfortable shepherding rather than controlling?

Are you acutely aware of your "J" (Judging) or your "P" (Perceiving) behavior—how does it manifest in group work?

Can you value some disorganization and a little emergence without letting things get entirely out of control?

V

When the Organization Isn't Ready to Support the Commitment

"No problem can be solved from the same
level of consciousness that created it."

ALBERT EINSTEIN

There may be times when the HR organization is ready to go with a group but there isn't enough support in the organization's leadership. Sometimes you won't know this until you get a group underway. It sure helps to do your due diligence up front to ensure leadership is involved, has input, and knows the commitment that is expected of the participants. One way to manage this is with an appreciative inquiry (AI) approach. In organizing with AI, we use the 4-D cycle, which includes Discover, Dream, Design and Destiny, and work it around a strategic topic. You might have other preferred models or approaches to assessment, and I encourage you to use what you're most comfortable with. The important thing is that you're organizing for clarity and success through discussing assumptions, beliefs, and desires early. With the collective wisdom of the appropriate stakeholders you will feel better about the readiness factor.

Some organizations have tried a variety of leadership development initiatives and have not been satisfied with outcomes. It is important to know about and learn from these experiences.

We talked about invitations earlier in Part 2, Chapter 2. To avoid future problems, make sure all participants have the dates as soon as possible and that they know they are expected to make every effort to attend all the sessions. You'll want both the participant and the manager aligned with these expectations. There are some managers who want to pull participants from group meetings for other meetings without considering if it is absolutely necessary. I learned too late into one group that an employee who missed three sessions was being pressured by her boss to attend other meetings. It wasn't really his fault. He didn't know what the group work was really about as he became her manager after the group got started. She hadn't thought to have a good sit-down with him to explain her commitment and it evaded HR to fill him in as well. Missing three group sessions meant that she lost out on important experiences, discussions, and contributions, and inconvenienced her peer coach and other dyad partnerships. With her manager's apparent lack of interest, her own interest was waning. In another instance an individual never presented to the group with a dyad partner because of late call-outs. This left her partners responsible to carry the full load and gave her a bad reputation.

On the other hand, I never would have tried videoconference groups had an HR client not said that it was her dream to include the entire organization. We co-created how it would work, got the green light from her leadership, and in the end all were delighted with the outcomes. The company further supported the initial commitment by making it possible for me to make one European trip per group. That enabled me to meet as many of the participants outside the U.S. who could come to the planned location. I combined the visit with running one of the monthly meetings while I was there. That brought more enthusiasm to the parts of the group at a distance.

"For me, this is a familiar image—people in the organization ready and willing to do good work, wanting to contribute their ideas, ready to take responsibility, and leaders holding them back, insisting that they wait for decisions or instructions. The result is dispirited employees and leaders wondering why no one takes responsibility or gets engaged anymore. In these troubled times, we don't need more command and control; we need better means to engage everyone's intelligence in solving challenges and crises as they arise."

MARGARET WHEATLEY

A good experience like this happens when there is trust and maturity among the leaders who are making such decisions. That's not to say that everyone has to be creative and agreeable—we all have defenses and we all use them. But if someone is overly guarded or too egotistical, it will create difficulty and potentially sabotage the initiative. This could be a sponsor, HR, a participant, or a manager of a participant. At this level in most organizations, these individuals have already been weeded out. But if you see it in the planning stages, it could be a warning sign.

Being open to possibilities and the needs of an organization allows the leaders to also be open with you. Even though you come with a certain amount of expertise, you must always realize that you don't know everything. Organizations want to do well by their employees, but they do have parameters, concerns, and constraints. We also want to do well by the organization and will often be able to allay concerns and work with constraints. Overall, our mission is to provide good leadership development opportunities. We want to encourage, facilitate, and support growth and employee engagement. We want our clients to feel good about the partnership. And we want participants of our groups to know they've been chosen for this opportunity because they've earned it. It is a real vote of confidence on the part of leadership. They are all people who know it requires effort and intentionality to achieve new levels of capability. They are generally committed to continuous development, and most have a positive outlook. In other words, they feel the appreciation and are appreciative in return. They see opportunity where others might just see more work, and most are used to managing through difficulties to possibilities. They already know that "even the word obstacle is an obstacle."

Questions to consider

How will you determine the readiness of an organization for this kind of intervention?

Have you had the experience of receiving gentle nudges that the timing might not be right for a particular effort but ignoring it because your enthusiasm wanted to push forward?

If so, write down a few thoughts about why you wish you would have waited and how that might have promoted better outcomes.

_____

_____

_____

_____

_____

_____

_____

_____

_____

_____

_____

_____

_____

_____

_____

_____

_____

_____

Part IV

The Coach's Continuing Growth from Group Work

"The suffering that comes from useful work, and from the victory over real difficulties, brings with it those moments of peace and satisfaction which give the human being the priceless feeling that he has really lived his life."

C. G. JUNG

I

Strengthening Group Coaching Competencies

"...pay the most attention to the person using the tools, meaning oneself, rather than focusing on the design of the tool. An excellent tool in the hands of a struggling professional can do great damage while an imperfect tool in the hands of a true craftsperson can morph into an awesome impact at individual, team and organizational levels."

BEVERLY PATWELL & EDITH WHITFIELD SEASHORE,
TRIPLE IMPACT COACHING

Beyond the many benefits noted throughout this book, there are several important lessons that I gain through the groups that make the work interesting and rewarding. For example, I learn a great deal about the various aspects of business and systems and organizational life. I learn about Types® in the group setting. I learn how the Types® influence and communicate, how they suffer and struggle, and what they desire and are driven by. I learn about diversity within and among the Types®, around the world and within regions. Sometimes our differences may seem insurmountable, but we are also quite similar in our modern world needs, interests, and desires. And at a fairly basic level, all people want to contribute, to be appreciated, and to be heard. Some want to be liked, some want to be admired, some respected, and just a few want to be left alone.

I appreciate being committed to work that keeps me learning. I've contemplated which competencies are most important to coaching for more than 15 years. I started with clusters that frame the work of the coach through the main core coaching skills and then through subsets. These subsets include the interpersonal skills, intrapersonal skills (which I have emphasized most in this series because I feel they are critical to ethical working and a piece that is often minimized), problem-solving skills—which I use more in the work of consulting and organizational development, but do find they come in handy as a group coach and facilitator— and business skills (in addition to the business of coaching and being able to run one's own business). I've outlined these competencies here. You can argue if these are the *right* ones or if they are precise enough, but I think they cover the territory and give one a lot to consider when striving for increased competence in their role.

Core Coaching Competencies

- Commitment to ethical practice
- Engaging, influencing, contracting
- Skilled and certified in assessment and other appropriate tools
- Knowledge of human development and adult learning theory
- Facilitating the development conversation
- Setting group coaching objectives
- Goal setting and development planning with the individual
- Negotiating exercises and follow-through
- Supporting progress updates with the manager as appropriate to the contract and the individual
- Bringing the engagement to a close

Interpersonal Competencies

- Establishing trust and rapport
- Collaborating, co-creating
- Developing conscious and courageous conversations
- Being a facilitator of insight

- Effective listening (including active listening, using empathy)
- Thoughtful questioning
- Giving feedback (providing both support and challenge)
- Managing confidentiality
- Maintaining integrity
- Having respect for diversity of all kinds
- Being learning agile
- Responding effectively to conflict

Intrapersonal Competencies

- Insight into one's Self*
- Understanding one's values
- Integration of new and continuous learning
- Possessing self-worth and self-confidence
- Managing your emotions and behaviors

Problem-Solving Competencies

- Researching and diagnosing
- Identifying and analyzing alternatives
- Decision making
- Efficient response time

Business Competencies

- Some knowledge of the industry one is working in
- Knowledge of the business and its leadership
- Organizational savvy
- Client management
- Systems perspective

*Includes becoming authentic through the practices of journaling and mindfulness meditation.

When you have your own business, you don't always get a lot of direct feedback. You can use these competencies as a checklist or yearly evaluation tool in order to determine your strengths and weaknesses in these areas and set some goals for improvement in the year ahead.

But always remember, the inner work is the most crucial. There are many powerful forces within the psyche that I have merely scratched the surface on because we can only know them when we take that deep dive and experience them for ourselves. While many will put off making the inner journey, this is the work that really matters for developing an authentic life, a life that impacts the level of contribution you make, and the legacy you leave.

Observing, Examining, Learning, Becoming

The *Red Book* series has been my journey to waking up, to gaining more consciousness, to freeing the witness within to see what the egoic self cannot and to providing thoughtful direction for my next steps. Group work has been of particular use to this effort. While you don't get a lot of direct feedback on your performance, you do receive invaluable feedback on yourself. In what other situation can I find 10 mirrors to provide feedback and insight for me. If I find one person annoying and another person overwhelming, that's feedback. If I have empathy for someone or am particularly fond of an individual, that's

> "We meet ourselves time and time again in a thousand disguises on the path of life."
>
> C.G. JUNG

feedback. If I find a participant disturbing in some way, that too is feedback. When I step into a group, I get immediate feedback if I choose to be aware and listen. I especially want to pay attention to any patterns to my judgments. For example, am I bothered by all people of a same Typology? Yes, I can say, I've definitely had that experience. It has forced me to look at what it points to that I dislike in myself and find ways to accept it or work on it. Of course, the more a person has an impact on me, the more important it is for me to get to work on understanding why and taking responsibility for what I find. That's the work of wholeness. While we cannot expect to ever find completion in ourselves, it is the journey toward it that enables us to become better human beings and better practitioners.

While I do believe in this kind of reflection and the opportunities to further develop skills, I also believe in just being—letting go and being mindful of the energies and feelings within me, without judging them, without always being reactive. In reflecting on what is reactive, Joseph Goldstein and Jack Kornfield, say:

> Our minds are reactive: liking and disliking, judging and comparing, clinging and condemning. Our minds are like a balance scale, and as long as we're identified with these judgments and preferences, likes and dislikes, wants and aversions, our minds are continually thrown out of balance, caught in a whirlwind of reactivity. It is through the power of mindfulness that we can come to a place of balance and rest. (Kornfield 2012)

This may be the hardest part, not beating up on yourself, not striving for perfection. Taking time for mindfulness meditation helps us to keep perspective, to value all that happens and all that we can learn from it. Allowing for nonjudgment, even if momentarily, gives us a broader perspective and appreciation for what is happening within us so that we can be thoughtful about and authentic with our next action. This is where our real power comes from: recognizing our shadow and choosing our response—projecting more of the positive, enabling us to meet the challenges before us. And mindfulness provides us with the presence to develop effective rapport with our clients—to be receptive and present.

> "Everything that irritates us about others can lead us to an understanding of ourselves."
>
> C.G. Jung

If organizations and global economies are going to truly work toward greater advancement, then a higher level of consciousness individually and collectively is a necessity. By emphasizing a safe environment in the group, we allow participants to practice being authentic so they can

"Truly, the greatest gift you have to give is that of your own self-transformation."

Lao Tzu

project that authenticity in other settings. In this way we foster this consciousness both in others and ourselves. This shows up as a confidence that brings with it a new level of creativity and collaboration to our work in the world.

Questions to consider

Which are your strongest competencies for this work?

What one or two competencies would you like to work on in support of your effectiveness with group work?

How will you go about doing that development work?

Is there a small nagging voice coming from your psyche that is trying to be heard relative to something your ego would rather ignore?

In Conclusion

As I mentioned above, the writing of this series along with the inner work that I have been doing over the last 15 years continues to raise my consciousness and my curiosity. There is some internal drive that makes me want to make sense of the human experience, but, of course, I know that comes from wanting to understand *my* experience. At this stage, I particularly enjoy helping people at that intersection of having meaningful work and living a meaningful life, likely driven by *my* desire to have meaningful work and a meaningful life.

As I continue the work of meaning making for my life, I reach for new ways to develop and transcend my ego. I've started to do some work in education and in faith-based organizations, as they require a slightly different approach—new sensitivities, new paradigms. These experiences align well with my core values and are making use of my tertiary and inferior functions.

It is not only leadership development and our corporate cultures that are experiencing a great deal of change; faith-based organizations are also struggling with survival and how to reinvent themselves. But perhaps in answer to Jung's question, there *are* schools for 40-year-olds. Perhaps, our churches are the place where people could learn to live into their midlife needs, providing support for and making the transformation to meaningful living accessible. And perhaps group work, too, can be the impetus for this kind of change—teaching us all how to have meaningful work and meaningful lives.

To conclude this work of bringing Jung's ideas into the current times, into the world of work, and specifically into group coaching, I will let Jung have the last word:

> "What is it, in the end, that induces a man to go his own way and to rise out of unconscious identity with the mass as out of swathing mist? Not necessity, for necessity comes to many, and they all take refuge in convention. Not moral decision, for nine

times out of ten we decide for convention likewise. What is it, then, that inexorably tips the scales in favor of the *extra-ordinary*? It is what is commonly called *vocation*: an irrational factor that destines a man to emancipate himself from the herd and from its well-worn paths. True personality is always a vocation and puts its trust in it as in God, despite its being, as the ordinary man would say, only a personal feeling. But vocation acts like a law of God from which there is no escape. The fact that many a man who goes his own way ends up in ruin means nothing to one who has a vocation. He must obey his own law, as if it were a daemon whispering to him of new and wonderful paths. Anyone with a vocation hears the voice of the inner man: he is *called*."

"The Development of Personality,"
Collected Works, C.G. Jung Vol 17

Training in the IGC Process

I am available to guide others in learning the Insight Group Coaching process. I believe we need many more skilled coaches and facilitators who are interested in doing the work of developing conscious leadership. This requires a commitment to inner work—a readiness and a desire by the individual to learn and work in a deeper, more psychically aware way. It requires time for gaining self-knowledge through journaling, mindfulness, and other reflective exercises. If you feel called to this work and wish to discuss what the customized training or an introductory workshop would involve, please send some brief notes outlining your interest and your background to Janet@leadersinsight.com.

Appendix

Coaching with an Analytical Framework
aligned with Jung's framework for analysis

ASPIRATION

Why do you want to engage in coaching? What are you wanting to do better, or be more effective at? What are your personal goals? Professional goals? What is your purpose? What does your manager think? What does HR think? Have you had a 360° assessment and what does it suggest? What do you aspire to? How have your aspirations led you to where you are today? Aspirations vs. inspirations? Rules of engagement (ie: confidentiality).

ASSESSMENT

Gather data through assessments; analyze and review with client; finalize development plans and connect with client sponsor. Assessment provides an opportunity for clarification and insight on "you" and a language for expressing yourself more fully. While most clients know themselves to some degree, much of the real insight has not been brought to light; elucidation is necessary where the point of fixation arises.

COACHING

Sessions with client where support and challenge are utilized to develop new skills and insights. Rapport is continuously developed through listening and clarification. We challenge the client to see the situation more clearly and ask questions from our own insights. Updates with manager or HR are intermittent as requested or appropriate. Plans are modified to enable the best outcomes.

TRANSITION

Closing out the process with the client in order to transfer them back to the full support of the system – manager, HR, and stakeholders. This is a time for celebration. New habits have been formed, new perspectives and attitudes adopted and a more resilient leader is ready to get back to the business of leading in a fully focused and confident way. However, not without a plan for continuing their development and ongoing insights in some thoughtful way.

CONFESSION

Recounting the truth of the moment; getting it out – giving voice to issues, concerns, realities. The act of having some trusted other hear your realities. Abreaction (Wikipedia 1/20/12) is a psychoanalytical term for reliving an experience in order to purge it of its emotional excesses; a type of catharsis. Sometimes it is a method of becoming conscious of repressed traumatic events.

ELUCIDATION

"While the cathartic method restores to the ego such contents as are capable of becoming conscious and should normally be components of the conscious mind, the process of clearing up the transference brings to light contents which are hardly ever capable of becoming conscious in that form. This is the cardinal distinction between the stage of confession and the stage of elucidation."

EDUCATION

New habits are won because of exercise and this requires education. "The patient must be drawn out of himself into other paths, which is the true meaning of education, and this can only be achieved by an educative will." The analyst may share a variety of thoughts and ideas allowing the patient to stretch, challenge and enlarge their world.

TRANSFORMATION

The doctor–patient relationship is very important to the outcomes. "For two personalities to meet is like mixing two different chemical substances: if there is any combination at all, both are transformed." The analyst must be open to influence in order to have influence in the analytic relationship. With this mutuality insights occur for both parties and they are transformed by the experience.

Steinwedel's CAF model/process

Jung's analysis model/process

References

Adams, Kathleen. 2018. "Center for Journal Therapy." [Web site], Last Modified July 30, 2013. journaltherapy.com.

Ballas, Paul, DO and Fraser, Marianne, MSN, RN. 2018. "Journaling for Mental Health." [website]. University of Rochester Medical Center, Last Modified 2018, accessed 12/9/2018.

Barker, Cara. 2001. *World weary woman: her wound and her transformation* Toronto: Inner City Books. Individuation and personal growth.

Bentz, Valerie Malhotra. 1989. *Becoming mature: childhood ghosts and spirits in adult life*. New York: Aldine de Gruyter.

Brown, Brene. 2012. *Daring greatly: how the courage to be vulnerable transforms the way we live, love, parent and lead*: Gotham Books.

Corey, Marianne Schneider and Gerald 1997. *Groups: process and practice*. Fifth ed: Brooks/Cole Publishing company.

Hecht, Justin B. 2011. "Becoming who we are in groups: one Jungian's perspective." *GROUP* 35 (2):151-165.

Hollis, James. 2005. *Finding meaning in the second half of life*. New York: Gotham Books.

Jung, C. G. 1960. *The structure and dynamics of the psyche*. Translated by R. F. C. Hull. Edited by executive editor William McGuire, Sir Herbert Read, M.D. Michael Fordham, M.R.C.P. and PH.D. Gerhard Adler. second ed. 18 vols. Vol. 8, *Bollingen Series XX*. Princeton Princeton University Press. Collected Works. Original edition, "The Stages of Life" (1930).

Jung, C. G. 1963. *Mysterium Coniunctionis*. Translated by R. F. C. Hull. Edited by Sir Herbert Read, M.D. Michael Fordham, M.R.C.P. and PH.D. Gerhard Adler, William McGuire, Executive Editor. second ed. 18 vols. Vol. 14, *Bollingen XX*. Princeton Princeton University Press.

Jung, C. G. 1971. *Psychological types*. Translated by H. G. Baynes (with revision by R. F. C. Hull). Edited by executive editor William McGuire, Sir Herbert Read, M.D. Michael Fordham, M.R.C.P. and PH.D. Gerhard Adler. 18 vols. Vol. 6, *Bollingen Series XX*. Princeton: Princeton University Press.

Kornfield, Joseph Goldstein and Jack. 2012. *Seeking the heart of wisdom: the path of insight meditation*. Boston & London: Shambhala.

Neal, Craig and Patricia. 2011. *The art of convening: authentic engagement in meetings, gatherings and conversations*: Berrett-Koehler Publishers, Inc.

Riga. 1999-2017. "Riga Gestalt Institute." Accessed 11/12/18. www.gestalt.lv.

Schein, Edgar. 1988. *Process consultation: its role in organization development.* 2 ed. Vol. 1. NY: Addison-Wesley.

Sharp, Daryl. 1987. *Personality Types.* Toronto: Inner City Books.

Stein, Murray. 1998. *Jung's map of the soul.* Chicago: Carus Publishing.

Warner, C. Terry. 1997. Intellectual foundations of Arbinger consulting and training. The Arbinger Company.

Whyte, David. 2019. "Gratefulness: Life as wholehearted journey." A network for grateful living, accessed February 3, 2019.

Woodman, Marion. 1982. *Addiction to perfection.*Toronto: Inner City Books.

Index

About Janet S. Steinwedel, PhD

As President of Leader's Insight, an Executive Coaching and Leadership Effectiveness Consultancy, Dr. Steinwedel works with a broad range of leaders on developing conscious and authentic leadership in industries including pharmaceuticals, health care, financial services, insurance, engineering, communications, retail, hospitality, education and faith-based organizations. Janet works from what she refers to as an "analytical framework," stemming from her studies and experiences with analytical psychology, which enables her to support transformational learning in her clients. Additionally, she devotes time to coaching coaches—supporting other coaches with their personal and professional development.

Janet is an adjunct professor and speaker. She enjoys travel, golf, swimming and time with family and friends.

www.LeadersInsight.com
Twitter: SteinwedelJanet
Facebook: The Golden Key to Executive Coaching

www.ingramcontent.com/pod-product-compliance
Lightning Source LLC
Chambersburg PA
CBHW031435270326
41930CB00007B/711